The
Manager's
Toolbox

Management Tools
You Need to Succeed

Mark Kelly

Thresher Press

Thresher Press
22365 El Toro Road, #344
Lake Forest, CA 92630

First Edition

Publisher's Cataloging in Publication
(Prepared by Quality Books Inc.)

Kelly, Mark, 1947-
    The manager's toolbox : Management tools you need to succeed / Mark Kelly.
    p. cm.
    ISBN 0-9655417-0-3

    1. Management. 2. Employees--Training of. I. Title.

HD31.K45 1997   658.4
                              QBI96-40675

Printed in the United States of America
May 1997

For:

John Toups,
who gave me the opportunity
to learn from my mistakes;

The members of the
1971-72 Clarkston High School soccer team,
who endured my first real attempt at management;

Sheryl Kelly, my daughter,
who taught me the true meaning
of sharing and caring.

THE MANAGER'S TOOL BOX

Contents

ONE

Some Thoughts on Retooling

TWO

"We are what we repeatedly do. Excellence, then, is not an act, but a habit."

THREE

"Managers delegate. Technicians do the work of their team members."

FOUR

"What we've got here...is a failure... to communicate."

NINE

"Passionate team members are your strongest catalysts for change."

TEN

"When the sun comes up, the lion knows he has to outrun the slowest gazelle...

When the sun comes up, the gazelle knows he has to outrun the fastest lion."

ELEVEN

"Water maintains no constant shape."

ONE

Some thoughts on retooling.

THE IMPOSSIBLE

Have you ever done 'the impossible' - not a seemingly inhuman physical feat such as lifting a car off of an injured person, but an achievement which no one thought could be accomplished?

Have you ever successfully led a group of people on an impossible effort for a sustained period of time?

I have been faced with two situations in my lifetime which required the sustained efforts and sacrifices of many people to successfully achieve what others believed to be impossible.

In the early 1970's I became the head coach of a high school soccer team (The Champagne Kids) in the suburbs of Atlanta. The team had finished near the bottom of their league's standings during the previous season.

This group of teenagers, a mixture of the recently emerging 'soccer kids' and renegades from the football team, had it in their minds that they were going to excel.

At first they thought I was crazy when they had to practice with tennis balls and play a somewhat outdated formation which I had learned during my junior high school days in New Jersey.

After a few early season successes a bond was formed which brought out the best in the team. Eventually they were able to knock off the defending state champion (undefeated in nearly three years) and become known as the best team in the state of Georgia.

What did it take for this group of fourteen to seventeen year old boys to achieve what was thought to be impossible?

- •A goal.
- •A plan of attack.
- •A zealous commitment to achieving the impossible.
- •The recognition of small successes.
- •Follow through.
- •The right tools.

GARDENING

Most of you perform some basic tasks in your spare time. When you make small repairs around the house, change the oil in your family automobile or plant and cultivate the landscape surrounding your home, one thing becomes evident in maximizing your success.

You have to have the right tools.

Have you ever tried to mow your lawn with a pair of scissors or weed your garden with a fork? These activities would require a great deal of effort and yield little or no success.

Many managers put forth tremendous energy each day which yields similar small rates of success because they, too, aren't using the right tools.

You have been successful because you developed methods for going about your work, whether through personal trial and error, formal management training or, as is true in many situations, a combination of both. You have also been able to learn from your organization and team members. Have they taught you the right things?

Is your organization or team functioning at its peak level of performance? Would the productivity and profitability of your team be enhanced if you could introduce and implement new tools to improve your teamwork, accountability, communication, planning and goals?

Be the catalyst for change.

1. You can be the instrument for positive change within your area of responsibility by understanding and utilizing the correct tools.

2. Show your peers and team members a better way to do things.

3. Help create an environment which fosters greater individual and team success.

TWO

"We are what we repeatedly do. Excellence, then, is not an act, but a habit."

Aristotle

WHAT MATTERS

If you want to be successful you must understand and differentiate between what really matters and what matters very little.

You may be familiar with concepts such as 'elements critical to success' or 'concentrating on the vital few'. Regardless of the terminology you prefer to use, the important thing is to stay focused upon 'what matters'.

Try this exercise. You have been on the road for the past four days. You return to your office to find a two foot stack of memos, mail and faxes on your desk - plus seventeen electronic mail messages on your computer.

What are you going to do?

Consider the five keys to prioritizing before you start working on each of the items in your information backlog.

1. **Does it require a response or action?** Some items are sent for informational purposes, some solicit a decision, and others require that a task be performed.

2. **When do you need to respond or act?** A due date or return date may be noted; otherwise, use your best judgment.

3. **What is the penalty for not responding on time?** Will you or your organization be put at risk if the return date is missed?

4. **What is the benefit from responding on time?** Is there an opportunity or an advantage to be gained by meeting the deadline?

5. **Can someone else do it?** If so, who?

Review these memos, faxes and messages. Sort each one according to what you are going to do.

1. Do it (respond or act) now.
2. Throw it away immediately.
3. Save it for future reading.
4. Schedule the response or action for a specific day or time of day.
5. Give it to someone else.

This simple exercise is a first step in helping you prioritize your daily activities.

Now you are ready to use your prioritizing skills on the more global aspects of 'what matters'. Look at the longer term projects for you and your team. Categorize these activities on the prioritizing matrix.

PRIORITIZING MATRIX

	This Week	This Month	This Quarter
•Most Important			
•Important			
•Little Importance			

This tool will help you clearly establish 'what matters' and keep your team focused on the big picture. It provides you with a clear perspective on your greater, longer term 'vital factors' and 'critical success factors' for running a successful operation.

**Know 'what matters' today and
'what matters' for tomorrow.**

A MOMENT OF CLARITY

The most frustrated managers I meet are those who have achieved some form of business 'stardom' through their own personal abilities prior to assuming management roles.

They have difficulty understanding why their new positions seem to yield slower rates of success than they experienced in the past.

If you share this feeling you probably haven't come to terms with the basic difference between individual achievement and group success.

The rules changed when you became a manager.

What you achieved as an individual is no longer good enough for your new responsibilities.

Your performance will be measured from this day forth in terms of how your team functions rather than what you are able to do by sheer personal effort and will power.

You will succeed or fail on the strength of your cross-personal skills.

1.   You can't be a strong delegator if you don't have a team of people who understand and accept delegation.

2.   You can't effectively manage your time if you don't build an environment in which everyone subscribes to and works on better time management.

3.   You can't communicate effectively unless your team members and peers are using the same parameters for listening to each other and getting their thoughts through.

4.   You can't create and implement a meaningful strategic plan without the participation and authorship of your team members and peers.

5.   You can't hold your team members accountable for their actions if you have failed to negotiate individual and group goals that are personal, important and consistent with the goals of the organization.

**If you choose to operate in a void
you are a technician,
not a manager.**

BRAINSWARMING

You just received a frantic call from one of your customers. The customer described a constant problem with a piece of production equipment which he purchased from your company within the last two months. You must come up with the best possible solution and get back to him as soon as feasible. What do you do next?

Gather up some of your team members (two to five will do), get out your flip chart easel and brainswarm.

1. Who's in charge?

Someone needs to take responsibility for the team's success. This is usually the person who knows the most about the current situation or problem - in this case, it's you. You become the designated facilitator to manage the team through the brainswarming process.

2. What's the problem?

You need to clearly and succinctly describe the situation or problem. What happened? When? What history do you have regarding the problem? What 'fixes' have been tried to date? What did you tell the customer?

3. What do we want to accomplish?

Define and explain what you are trying to achieve. State this in terms of how many solutions you should create (one will frequently be sufficient) and how much time you want to spend. In this situation - solving your customer's equipment problem - you are looking for the single best solution you can create in fifteen minutes.

4. What do you think?

Now it's time to swarm. Record your team's first, last, best, craziest and every other idea on the flip chart. Reject nothing. There is no such thing as a stupid idea when you are brainswarming. Encourage creativity.

5.   What are we going to do?

Work through the ideas listed on the flip chart. Use all of the time you have set aside. Narrow the possibilities down to three solutions, explore these in detail and select the single best answer.

6.   Who's going to do it?

Knowing what you need to do is only half of the battle, but it frequently enables you to determine who is going to complete the work. Be specific.

Make sure the team member who agrees to complete the task is clear on what the solution should look, sound and feel like.

7.   When will it be completed?

The person who will perform the job must have a clear understanding of when the tasks are to be completed. Use 'not later than' dates, or **'NLTs'**.

Record your action steps in the **'what, who and when'** format.

WHAT	WHO	WHEN
•		
•		
•		

THE TEXAS FOUR STEP

Would you benefit by having a simple framework to help you solve the problems and projects that you face each day?

The Texas Four Step was initially developed for the strategic planning process. It was subsequently identified as a meaningful tool for a number of managerial and organizational challenges and problem solving efforts.

1. **Establish the benchmark.**

   Where are you now? What is the starting point for the project? What has happened to date to create the problem you are facing?

   This is the first step in clearly identifying the problem or precisely understanding the nature of the project at hand.

2. **Set goals.**

   What are you or your team trying to achieve? Be specific. When do you want to achieve your goals? Set dates.

3. **Create strategies.**

   What plans of attack can you develop to reach your goals? Generate a list of action steps, determine the person who will be accountable for achieving each action step and specify the agreed upon completion date for each step.

4. **Monitor results.**

   Determine how each activity will be measured and documented. Establish scheduled milestone meetings to follow up on the strategies and action steps.

GET TOGETHERS

I often ask new clients for copies of the notes or minutes from their last three management or team meetings. I receive an array of responses to this request.

1.   "What meetings?" (forty percent of the time).

2.   "We have meetings, but we don't keep official notes" (another thirty percent).

3.   Minutes containing rambling narratives of what was discussed, with non-existent actions to be taken (about twenty-five percent).

4.   Action oriented minutes, with accountability and completion dates for tasks (maybe five percent!)

If you want to develop a strong team which communicates and works together you must hold team meetings which are oriented toward action and accountability. Don't hold get togethers!

A get together is an exercise where members of a group meet to discuss everything, argue about most things and accomplish nothing.

More time is wasted in the workplace today through poorly managed team meetings than any other activity.

If you hold a meeting attended by five managers whose pay averages $20.00 per hour, you are spending $100.00 in salaries alone for each hour of the meeting.

If it takes you three hours to accomplish one hour worth of value, you have wasted $200.00 in important management time. And you are doing this to the same managers who fret over minutely small swings in productivity percentages on the production floor.

Wasted time equals wasted dollars.

"A" TEAMS

Every team you manage should be focused upon accountability and achievement. Your accountability teams, or "A" teams, must know how to maximize the results from the time you spend together in meetings.

"A" Team meetings focus upon four basic activities.

1. Make decisions.

2. Create actions.

3. Establish accountability.

4. Set milestones and completion dates.

If you are not planning to accomplish something of significance, don't waste your team's time, and yours, by conducting a meaningless meeting.

Have a specific purpose before you schedule a team meeting. Don't subject your team members to the tedium of staring at each other for endless hours of talk, self-gratifying monologues and personal info-commercials.

1. Create a meeting agenda containing specific time periods and stick to the agenda.

2. Establish a team facilitator to ensure that the agenda is followed.

3. Meet regularly at predetermined times to ensure that all team members set their other activities and appointments to avoid scheduling conflicts.

4. The minutes of. each meeting must be clear, simple, documented and 'to the point'.

5. Distribute meeting minutes to any and all other interested parties. This includes every person who attended each meeting, their managers and anyone else who needs to know what decisions were made during your meetings.

Use this worksheet as the template for recording the minutes of your meetings.

MEETING MINUTES WORKSHEET

Team Members:
Date:
Distribute to:

WHAT   **WHO**   **WHEN**

-
-
-
-
-
-

Standups.

If you need to hold short informational meetings on a daily or frequent basis, try 'standups'. Conduct these meetings in rooms with no chairs.

One of my clients uses this format for daily fifteen minute operational meetings which are necessary for matching customer orders with available resources.

Drive home the sense of urgency.

DIVING

I learned a valuable lesson recently concerning the need for consistently applying fundamentals for survival and success.

One of my lifelong dreams was to become a scuba diver so, following my first open water discovery dive, I enrolled in the PADI Open Water diving certification program.

The training process involves tedious repetitions of a number of survival skills including mask clearing and regulator recovery.

When your regulator becomes dislodged from your mouth it tends to drift behind your shoulder; a simple technique called the arm-sweep method makes it relatively easy to locate and replace your mouthpiece to resume breathing.

Our class practiced the arm-sweep over and over until it became second nature to us in various diving conditions.

I ran into Ed at Miami International Airport about four months after he and I had completed our training and certification program. Ed was returning home from a dive trip on San Salvador Island in the Bahamas. He told me about a diving experience with a young man who was on his first deep water dive.

When Ed's dive group reached a depth of about eighty-five feet the young man panicked and became disoriented. As Ed approached the young man to provide assistance, the youth grabbed Ed's regulator mouthpiece and yanked it loose.

Because Ed had repeatedly practiced the arm-sweep recovery method in our training classes he automatically relocated and replaced his mouthpiece without giving it a second thought.

Know the 'have to dos', and do them all of the time.

Every industry and business has unique 'have to dos', or fundamentals, that must be carried out consistently and thoroughly in order to achieve success.

In the restaurant business, you must 'serve your hot food hot and your cold food cold'.

In the vending business, your machines must be 'C,F & W, or clean, filled and working', in order to maintain your customers and make a profit.

What are the 'have to dos' in your business?

Do you make snap decisions? Are you criticized for taking too long to make decisions?

If one of these questions applies to you then you fall into one of the two main categories of complaints I hear from employees about their managers.

How can you fix this problem? One helpful approach is to look at each decision in terms of whether it is revocable or irrevocable.

A revocable decision is a decision that, once made, can be changed or voided with little or no impact on the results of the organization. An example of a revocable decision would be something as simple as assigning cubicle space for your inside sales staff.

Make revocable decisions quickly.

An irrevocable decision is a decision that, once it is made, sets a course for the organization that is very difficult to change or nullify without resulting in a strong, negative operational or financial impact.

An irrevocable decision that many successful organizations eventually face is the decision to purchase land and build a new facility. This decision frequently involves increased borrowing, a decrease in cash flow, an increase in operating expense or some meaningful amount of operational downtime.

The impact of making quick, poorly thought out decisions in facility changes can be great enough to put your company out of business.

Think through
your irrevocable decisions.

SPEED

One of my clients recently attended a seminar on the business climate we face as we prepare to enter the next century. The key point he came away with was what the presenter called the 'Three C's for the 21st Century' - change, complexity and competition.

The key element in addressing and successfully facing up to these 'Three C's' is the speed with which business is being, and will be, conducted as we approach the year 2000.

If you wait for others to show you the way you will feel like a flat-footed cornerback in a football game against San Francisco's Jerry Rice - left in the dust!

Generate speed, don't respond to it.

You are limiting yourself if you believe that the expression 'haste makes waste' is still applicable to the way you run your business. Haste is a critical element in your ability to lead your group toward your objectives. You and your team must learn how to do things quickly and accurately.

A friend of mine told me that the most important measure of performance is time. He said you need to maximize your return on hours, not on investment.

Maximize your 'return on hours' by maintaining your focus on time.

You need to constantly examine every facet of your business and every available tool at your disposal to optimize your utilization of time. The old credo of 'do it right the first time' will have a new postscript as we approach the 21st century.

Do it right the first time - and do it fast.

THREE

**"Managers delegate.
Technicians do the work of
their team members."**

From a friend

GAS STOVE MEMORIES

Many children learn a valuable lesson when they become old enough to reach the top of a gas stove.

Driven by innocence and curiosity, they make an attempt to grab that intriguing flame coming out of the gas burner and zap - a tearful awakening occurs.

If you approached your first opportunity at delegating with the same degree of innocence and curiosity, you probably got burned then, too.

Your response to this failed attempt at delegation most likely paralleled the child's reaction to the gas stove encounter - 'I'm never going to try that again'.

Learn a better way.

If you 'got burned' the first time you tried to delegate to one of your team members, you probably didn't know what you were doing.

Delegation is a cross-personal function. It requires ground rules that are understood and accepted by every person on your team.

You can't delegate in a void.

1.   Teach your team members how to delegate.

2.   Teach your team how to receive delegation.

3.   Create a group-wide tool for greater excitement and performance by all of your team members.

HIGHEST AND BEST USE

Property revaluation companies are in business to provide new property valuations, on a mass basis, to taxing jurisdictions (cities, municipalities and counties) as the foundations for assessing real estate taxes.

The key task in property valuation is establishing a real estate parcel's worth at its 'highest and best use'.

Shouldn't you, and every member of your team, be working at your 'highest and best use'?

Take an inventory of your activities.

Take a tough look at what you do each day to determine the value you add to your team and your organization. Do your activities fall in line with the amount of money you are earning?

Are you reaching down into your organization to find things to do or are you reaching up to perform at your highest and best use?

Look at your job description. If it has been properly written your job description will provide you with the elements of work which are of value to your organization. How much of your time is devoted to these valued activities and responsibilities?

Review the activities of your team members.

Are you performing some of their tasks? Are they performing some of their employees' tasks?

Analyze what each person on your team should be doing. Create an environment where each team member is reaching up and out to deliver the best value to the organization.

THE DUMP

You are the manager of a division of a large corporation, you are buried in day to day problems and you just received a package from your manager at corporate. You haven't had a chance to look at the package, you have to get it turned around in thirteen days, so you decide to try that 'delegation thing'.

You call in Charley, your extremely hard working, intelligent manager of accounting/human resources/legal/whatever. The meeting goes something like this.

You: Charley, I just received this package from corporate. I haven't had a chance to look at it and it has to be back to corporate in thirteen days.

I know you are busy, too, but my only option is to give it to you and let you do the best job you can do. I need your finished report back in twelve days.

Charley: Okay. I'll do the best I can.

Did you delegate that project to Charley? No, you dumped it!

There is a vast difference between delegating and 'dumping'. In order to delegate there are some subtle actions that must take place. Here are three things you could have done to turn your 'dumping' into delegating.

1.   **Provide a charter.**

You have to know enough about the task you are delegating to set the parameters. Let Charley know what you expect the finished product to look, sound and smell like when it is finished.

2. **Set milestones.**

Set interim time checks to monitor Charley's progress. This allows Charley optimal leeway to proceed without having to worry about getting off track.

It gives Charley the opportunity to grow and be as creative as possible without letting the project get out of control. Establish the first review meeting for three days from now at a definite time and place. This step will also keep you off of Charley's back in the interim period.

3. **Relax.**

The project is not even on your agenda for the next three days!

POWER LIFTING

Your role as a manager requires that you constantly achieve results under the weight of increasing responsibility. If you've ever been to a gym which has a free weight area, you are probably familiar with those fifty and one hundred pound plates of weights used by the power lifters.

If you are like many other managers, you probably feel overloaded with the huge plates of weights from your own responsibilities. You are able to lift and carry these weights each day and still direct the efforts of the members of your team.

Some managers allow themselves to become encumbered with the additional weights of their managers who are unable, afraid or unwilling to make the decisions they are being paid to make.

Don't take on more weight than you can carry.

Your job is to coach your team members, to reinforce them, to foster their growth to be able to accept more weight, more responsibility, and more individual accountability for their actions.

1.   Help your team members understand what you must accomplish as their manager.

2.   Let your team members know what you expect from them.

3.   Negotiate and reconcile what you expect from each team member with what he or she wants and needs to achieve.

Your team members must accept their own responsibilities.

JUGGLING

The circus is full of performers who amuse and dazzle the audience - lion tamers, high wire aerialists, elephant trainers and clowns.

One of the most entertaining acts you see in the circus is performed by the jugglers.

How do they keep three or more balls, hammers, knives or flaming torches in the air? Hey, you do it every day as a manager!

A technician performs one task well.
A manager juggles multiple
tasks very well.

If your day requires juggling many balls or fires at one time, you should be happy to know that, as a manager, you are not alone.

Keep your focus on the concurrent tasks of your team members.

The art of management juggling requires team members who are able to do their parts in keeping many tasks and projects in the air at one time.

You can't do it all on your own.

Each ball or project or task which is in the air at one time must have a name assigned to it. The names on these tasks can't all be yours.

You have to know the disposition of each ball or project at any given time, but you do not have to perform each task.

Learn the art of vicarious juggling.

THE ANNUITY

Do you find that you neither have nor take the time during your day to devote to training your team members to take on some of your work load?

Most managers are very short sighted when it comes to teaching team members to pick up new tasks.

I can do it quicker myself.

You probably can do it quicker by yourself today, or this week, or this month. But if you teach someone else to perform that task it will get done each day, week or month with less of your personal time in the ensuing time periods.

Give some thought to the tasks you summarily perform over and over again. Are you the only person who can properly complete these tasks?

Make a time investment.

Do you put your money to work for you so that it can grow in the future? Why not do the same thing with your time?

1. Pick out something that takes you thirty minutes to complete on a monthly basis.   It may take you as much as one hour this month to teach one team member to perform the task. Now you have only invested an additional thirty minutes.

2. In the following month it might take you thirty minutes to meet with your team member to review performance on the task and provide your insights and ideas. At the end of the second month you are still only down thirty minutes.

3.   Month three. It only takes you ten minutes to review what your team member did this month. You are now only down ten minutes.

4.   From the fourth month through the twelfth month you utilize two minutes of your time to review your team member's work.

    You pick up twenty-eight minutes a month for these nine months, or a total of four hours and two minutes in the first year alone.

5.   In each ensuing year you save five hours and thirty-six minutes.

6.   If you do this with eight tasks you gain one full week per year.

Part of my work experience occurred in the field of accounting and finance. I take special notice of the behavior I observe when I visit with chief financial officers and other financial and accounting managers.

It is not uncommon for me to find financial executives hard at work creating and posting journal entries as regular functions of their jobs.

When I ask them why they are doing this, the frequent responses are 'I like to keep my hand in accounting' or 'this is something I always enjoyed doing'.

Don't dip back into the past.

Just because you used to perform a function years ago is no excuse for turning that task into today's comfort zone.

1. Keep track of what you are doing with your time each day.

2. How much time do spend performing tasks which should be done by other members of your team?

3. Identify these tasks. Give them to someone else.

4. Make the time investment to get these tasks off of your desk and onto someone else's desk.

5. Do something else with your time.

6. Work to your highest and best use.

Let your team members grow to create new opportunities for your own growth.

THE WORLD'S ONLY GENIUS

Your ego tells you that you are a pretty smart person. Just look at the success you have achieved so far!

Do you let your ego get in the way of delegating to your team members? If you need to get something done right, do you believe that you have to do it yourself?

Managers manage.
Team members get the job done.

If you do a good job of putting your team together, you should have more than adequate resources among your team members to delegate the important tasks to them.

Break the habit of being the best
performer on your team.

1. Select a task or project that you have always performed in the past.

2. Be specific on what you want the result to look, smell and feel like.

3. Don't be specific on what the result should actually be.

4. Set a deadline. Set milestones.

5. Monitor progress.

6. Acknowledge creativity during interim periods.

7. Recognize that the result is close to, or better than, any that you may have achieved.

Smile. You are delegating.

FOUR

"What we've got here...is a failure... to communicate."

A quote by the Louisiana prison captain (Strother Martin)
to the convict Luke (Paul Newman) from the movie
"Cool Hand Luke"

SAY SOMETHING NICE

There is a large hole-in-the-wall restaurant off of a side street next to Bally's Hotel and Casino in Las Vegas called, oddly enough, Batista's Hole-in-the-Wall.

A sign hanging on the entrance window - the only window in the place - proudly states:

"It'sa nice to be important, but it'sa more important to be nice."

Do you go out of your way to say something nice each day to the people who work around you? Why not?

• Are you too busy?

• Are you too caught up in the negative side of your days to see all of the positive actions that are happening around you?

• Have you managed to progress through your career without the benefit of fully developing all of your communication skills?

• Are you convinced that the people around you are supposed to do 'a good job' without any positive feedback from you?

Didn't anyone tell you that you must establish the tone and the environment for your team?

Everyone likes a compliment.

An important part of your role as manager is to create and foster a positive working atmosphere for your team members.

If you don't take the lead, someone else will. If you abdicate this management responsibility, your odds are only 50-50 that the person who fills this void will provide a positive and optimistic outlook.

Negative attitudes and comments travel further and faster than positive ones.

OPEN UP AND OUT

A friend of mine told me about a study which determined the methods people use to communicate in face to face meetings.

The three leading means of direct communication are body language, words and facial expressions. The study also measured the percentage of communication achieved by each of these three methods.

The results may surprise you. Forty-five percent of face to face communication is achieved through body language. Another forty-five percent is accomplished through facial expressions. Only seven percent of this direct form of communication is attributed to the spoken word.

I guess my mother was right when she told me, "It's not what you say, but how you say it, that counts."

Be aware of the messages you are sending when you communicate.

The successful communicator uses a blend of skills to open up the process of expression by all of the involved parties. Think of this technique as a form of ESP - Empathy, Sensitivity and Perspective.

1.   **Empathy.** Put yourself in the other person's shoes.

      What significance does the other person place upon your particular words or mannerisms?

2.   **Sensitivity**. What words or mannerisms by you will trigger either positive or negative reactions by the other person?

      Look for signs that indicate a defensive posture.   Correct the situation immediately if you create a hostile reaction.

3.   **Perspective.** Maintain your objectivity.

      Don't let defenses block the way to communication.

Early in my business career I worked for a manager who was known by his team members as Rambling Ron.

Ron was a brilliant tactician, a force within our industry and an empathetic leader, but the most frustrating thing about working for Ron was his inability to clearly communicate to his team what he wanted us to do.

When he initiated a discussion in a team meeting Ron would begin with a concrete thought and proceed to muddle things up by rambling on and on until, after about three minutes of absorbing Ron's monologue, the listeners would be completely confused.

At the conclusion of each meeting my fellow team members and I would conduct a private 'defogging' conference in an attempt to decipher exactly what point or points Rambling Ron was trying to make. Our 'defogging' success rate was about eighty percent.

Most of your success in communicating comes from not saying too much.

Your goal as a communicator is to get your point across with clarity and precision. You will succeed in reaching this goal if you are able to present your ideas by painting sharp mental pictures.

Organize your thoughts.

One of the keys to communicating with precision is to organize your thoughts into a series of bullet points. This technique is used frequently by public speakers.

When you listen to an effective luncheon or dinner speaker you will notice that the speaker is talking to the audience as opposed to reading a script to the group. The presenter is able to create an informal speaking atmosphere by expanding upon a short list of bullet, or topic, points.

Utilize this technique the next time you meet with one of your peers or team members. Establish in your own mind the two or three most important points you wish to make and deliver these points by creating acute mental images.

GET THROUGH

I heard a story during my college days about an aspiring writer who made a pilgrimage to Ernest Hemingway's home in the Bahamas.

The young man waited patiently on Hemingway's boat dock anxiously anticipating the return of his idol. When the famous outdoorsman alit from a day of fishing in the Gulfstream the hopeful writer seized his chance for an audience.

"Mr. Hemingway," he said, "what do I need to know to become a great writer?"

As the story goes, Ernest Hemingway responded by saying, "If you don't know big words, don't become a writer. If you know big words, don't use them."

You are not communicating if no one knows what you are talking about.

If you want to impress someone with your vocabulary you should write letters to David Frost.

Your responsibility as a manager is to make sure that each of your team members understands what you are trying to say.

Speak on the listener's level.

1. Break your ideas and requests down into the simplest forms possible.

2. This is an era of specialization. Every technical discipline has its own language. Translate specialized words and meanings into layman's terms.

3. Encourage team members to tell you when they don't understand what you are trying to communicate. Build an environment in which a lack of comprehension is intolerable.

Transmitters give out information. Communicators get through.

KISSINGER'S ACCENT

I recently watched a comedy special featuring Mort Sahl.

In this show Mort was telling a more than likely fictitious story about attending a White House dinner with General Alexander Haig. The keynote speaker at this function was Dr. Henry Kissinger. Part of Mort's conversation with the General went something like this.

Mort Sahl: Isn't it amazing that Henry Kissinger has been able to reach such lofty heights for someone who was born in a foreign country?

General Haig: You are mistaken, Mr. Sahl, Dr. Kissinger was born right here in the United States.

Mort Sahl: No, that can't be right. I thought he was born in Austria or Germany.

General Haig: That is a common misunderstanding.

Mort Sahl: Well, if that's the case, how come he has such a strong accent?

General Haig: That, Mr. Sahl, is the result of never having listened to anyone!

Learn how to listen when others are speaking.

Do you make these common listening mistakes?

1. You fail to focus on what's going on, right now, with the other person.

2. You feel that the other person has nothing to offer. In other words, you have already decided that you don't care what he or she has to say.

3. You assume you know what the other person is going to say.

TWO EARS, ONE MOUTH

Patricia had unlimited horizons for personal achievement in the property management industry.

I met her in one of my management development workshops and the accolades she received from her manager and peers were dampened by a nearly unanimous footnote: "Please teach her to avoid ending everyone else's sentences."

Patricia is one of those successful managers who always seems to be thinking one step ahead of everyone else. When others are talking too slowly Patricia automatically inserts her thoughts and ideas in a subconscious effort to supplement and complete their sentences.

You rarely learn something new when you are talking.

I was taught as a child that the only individuals in this world who are truly 'interesting' are the same people who are also 'interested'. How can you remain 'interested' and use your ears twice as often as you use your mouth when someone else is trying to communicate with you?

1. **Avoid personal interruptions.** Give the communicator your complete attention. Don't read your mail or telephone messages when someone is talking to you. Let the other person finish his or her thoughts.

2. **Eliminate external interruptions.** Activate your voice mail or have someone take your phone calls. Tell your secretary or 'gate keeper' that you don't wish to be disturbed.

3. **Concentrate on the speaker.** Establish how much time you wish to devote to the discussion. Communicate to the other person the amount time you wish to spend during the meeting. Avoid looking out of the window or at your watch.

Slow down and listen.

ACTIVE LISTENING

One of the ways you can improve your listening skills is to understand and appreciate the art of participating in a conversation without saying a single word.

Consummate listeners are able to encourage and take an active role when someone else is speaking by utilizing reinforcing body language and facial expressions.

Listen actively.

Active listening encompasses a wide spectrum of activities which ranges from silent reception to overt participation.

One end of the spectrum contains a skill which has been referred to as 'suspended' active listening. Suspended active listening allows you to involve yourself in the communication without actually speaking.

This form of active listening is subtle but very effective. It requires that you learn how and when to smile, nod and use other forms of non-verbal expression to play a supportive role when a colleague is trying to get a point across.

A more overt and participative form of active listening utilizes your direct interaction in 'closing the loop' with the speaker. This is the 'repeat after me' style of active listening.

If you are flying into a city to conduct a meeting with one of your team members, you may wish to use this 'participative' active listening skill. Example:

You: Hi, Ed. I'm coming in on American flight number 463 at two-thirty tomorrow afternoon. Will you be able to pick me up?

Ed: Yes, I will. I'll see you tomorrow at two-thirty at the gate for American flight number 463.

This 'closing of the loop' process ensures that you are getting your point across - and that you will have a ride from the airport!

"ADVANTAGE, RECEIVER"

One of the keys to becoming a competitive tennis player is learning how to position yourself - mentally, physically and geographically - for the return of your opponent's serve.

The greatest players possess not only the necessary skills but also the proper mental attitude to accept the delivery of the person across the net.

You have a similar responsibility when you are listening to someone who wishes to communicate with you.

As a listener you must adopt the 'proper mental attitude' for being attentive and for fostering communication.

Learn how to receive the other person's 'serve'.

1. Develop an atmosphere of acceptance. No one wants to communicate with you if you frequently reject what is being said.

    Show that you place importance on other's ideas. Don't interrupt the other person's speaking and thought processes unless you need immediate clarification.

2. Be aware of your body language and facial expressions. Create an 'openness of interest' to encourage the speaker.

    Avoid wearing your negative emotions on your face. Encourage others to express themselves by using supportive body language.

Great communicators are at their best when others are talking.

FIVE

"Time is vicious when you take it for granted."

Spoken by Bugsy Siegel (Warren Beatty)
in the movie "Bugsy"

A CAT ON YOUR BACK

During my last year in college I lived with two friends in a house that had been built for 'economy' during the 1920's in rural South Carolina.

The nights were cold in January...so cold that Jagger, our Siamese cat, would frequently sleep under the covers with one of us. Before classes each day we would congregate around the gas oven in the kitchen to warm up and drink our first cups of coffee.

One morning one of my roommates decided to play a trick on me. I had just come from the shower and, wrapped only in a towel, I leaned over to warm myself in front of the oven. Before I knew what was happening my roommate grabbed Jagger and tossed him onto my back.

Jagger was terrified. He proceeded to dig his claws into my back and hang on for dear life. I ran to my room, ripped Jagger off of my back and hurled him onto the bed. I wound up with four holes slashed into the corners of my backside - upper backside, fortunately.

How many cats are thrown on your back every day?

If you are like most managers you have an endless procession of peers and team members who attempt to rip cats off of their backs and throw them onto yours. Example:

Bob: Sandra, I need to make a decision on the Watertown proposal pricing this afternoon. Should I go with fixed prices or use cost plus a percentage profit?

Sandra: Let me think about it. I'll get back to you by noon.

Did Sandra take the cat?

Bob has successfully thrown the dreaded cat, or his responsibility, onto Sandra's back, forcing her to take the next step of making the decision.

How could Sandra have responded differently to deflect the cat off of her back?

Sandra: I'd like you to work up both options and bring them to me by one o'clock. Be prepared to discuss the pluses and minuses of both options and give your recommendation.

Sandra is forcing Bob to keep the cat on his back, where it belonged all along, and allowing Bob the opportunity to make a decision which he is being paid to make.

Sandra has prevented one more item from being added to her list of things to do and freed up her time to perform the tasks she is being paid to perform.

A WASTE OF TIME

I work with managers every day who feel overwhelmed and frustrated by the magnitude of tasks they are supposed to accomplish. I find it helpful to ask them, "How do you look at time?"

A sampling of answers:

> "I'm a slave to it!"
> "I don't have enough of it!"
> "I don't even have time to think about it!"

Most of you become so caught up in the 'tyranny of the urgent' that you are unable to take an objective look at the concept of time. You need to examine your ability to get things done. Put time into perspective.

Time is a resource.

Time is a far different asset than the other resources you manage each day. Why is time so unique?

Unlike production equipment, money, materials, people, research and development, buildings, land, or vehicles, time is a severely limited resource.

Time is not a commodity.

If I want to take the afternoon off and completely waste the rest of the day, I cannot donate those hours to you and give you a 30 hour day. In other words, you can't buy time, lend time or sell time.

Each of you are given twenty-four hours a day for seven days a week for four plus weeks a month for twelve months a year, and so forth, to do what you feel motivated to accomplish.

If you want to sleep all day, you have that right. But one thing is certain. You will never have the opportunity to relive the day that you choose to waste wrapped around your pillow.

Do you know how you spend your time?

LOGGING

If you are serious about making significant improvements in the way you utilize your time, try using the Texas Four Step.

Establish the benchmark.

1.   Log your time carefully and accurately each day. Use your Day-Timer, Franklin Planner or any other instrument you are comfortable with to keep a record of how you actually spend your time. Be honest and realistic.

2.   Take a few minutes prior to lunch and before you go home to log the activities that you undertook during each half day. Don't be afraid to record time that you feel was wasted due to interruptions or mindless daydreaming.

3.   Summarize your daily logs at the end of one week. This enables you to gain a clear grasp of your time benchmark, your stepping off point toward a better use of your time. Use the following worksheet to summarize your week.

WEEK ONE - THE BENCHMARK

Activities	Time Utilized	Percentage of Total Time
1.		
2.		
3.		
4.		
5.	_____	_____
Totals	_____	_____

TIME GOALS

Once you establish your time benchmark, you are ready to utilize this information to better manage your time in the future.

Set Goals.

Create answers to the following questions:

1. Does your time benchmark represent the best utilization of your day? Which activities should you add to the list? Which activities should you eliminate?

2. Which activities should take more of your time? Which activities should take less of your time?

Complete the following time goal worksheet.

WEEK TWO · GOALS

	Activities	Percentage of Total Time
1.		
2.		
3.		
4.		
5.		_____
	Totals	_____

TIME WARRIORS

You are not going to be able to 'wing it' when it comes to achieving real improvements in your time management. You need to have a plan of attack with thoroughly thought out strategies and action steps.

Create Strategies.

•Stay focused upon 'what matters'.

•Don't become overwhelmed by interruptions. Try a different approach when team members interrupt you looking for 'ready made' answers. Make them bring at least two alternative solutions.

•Plan your daily activities. Use the first fifteen minutes of each day, or the last fifteen minutes of the previous day, to list the things you need to accomplish. Include some time for unknown emergencies.

•Utilize your team members - delegate.

•Make a list of the top five strategies which you commit to implementing during the week. Write them down on the Strategies worksheet.

WEEK TWO - STRATEGIES
1.
2.
3.
4.
5.

RELOGGING

Let's see how you've done in your efforts to improve your management of time.

Monitor Results.

Repeat the logging process you utilized when you established your initial time management benchmark.

Keep your time management goals and strategies in mind as you conduct business every day.

WEEK TWO · RESULTS

Activities	Time Utilized	Percentage of Total Time
1.		
2.		
3.		
4.		
5.	_____	_____
Totals	_____	_____

ANNUAL CHECKUPS

Give yourself a periodic checkup.

Implement a time management checkup every six months or each year to ensure that you are still on track.

Repeat your time management program by logging, setting goals, strategizing and relogging to validate and verify that you are keeping those cats off of your back.

Log your time utilization within one to two months following a significant restructuring of your responsibilities.

Treat time as though it is as precious as your health.

SIX

"If you believe in nothing, you will fall for anything."

Anonymous

TEXTURE

The successful business wears its texture like a scent. This scent is easily detected when one spends any time around the members of the organization.

Texture embodies the core of your business. It defines your organization's personality and integrity.

Your team or organization requires a way of conducting business which governs how your people are expected to operate on a day to day basis.

Texture defines the essence of the organization. It creates an environment of pride and positive attitudes.

Texture is tangible. It is a concrete, living entity that pervades every aspect of a successful business. The viability and longevity of the business depends upon establishing and maintaining (and not losing!) the organization's 'way of doing things' as the business grows and new managers arrive.

Know what you want to be.

New managers and employees must understand and buy into the organization's texture. They must view the organization's 'way of doing things' as the foundation for meaningful growth.

Growth which contradicts the organization's texture will eventually create failure because the common thread which holds the business together will be lost.

What do you want or need to keep from the old way of doing business?

What do you want or need to change for a new way of doing business?

Learn how to blend the old with the new.

GONE GONE

When my daughter was beginning to learn how to speak she grabbed at certain expressions and repeated them whenever they remotely fit a given event or occasion. One of her first and favorite small word groups was, "Gone gone."

When her mother and I would leave her for the evening with a babysitter or her grandfather would make a coin disappear up his sleeve, she would shout, "Gone gone."

When a business forgets what it stands for or fails to educate new employees about the texture of the organization it frequently finds that its key customers are also 'Gone gone'.

Don't get fired by your customers.

A recent United Airlines television commercial focuses upon a business which is losing accounts because the company has forgotten the key elements of its success.

In an emotional early morning meeting the founder tells his sales staff something like this: "An old friend called to say he fired us. After twenty years (as a customer) he fired us. He said we used to do business face to face with a hand shake. Now we do business with phone calls and faxes."

The founder then hands out airplane tickets - this is, after all, an airline commercial - and reminds the sales representatives to rebuild personal relationships with the customers.

What the manager had failed to realize is that good judgment and sound business practices arise when the texture of the organization is clearly defined and communicated to each and every employee.

Keep you team focused upon your 'way of doing things'.

ETHICAL SUPERSTRUCTURE

Texture originates from the values of the founder in the initial stages of the organization and embodies what he or she stands for and what she or he believes is important.

Values are created by understanding what is good for you, what is bad for you, what you want to be involved in and what you want to avoid.

Values provide the basis for - and direct - the actions and results of a successful business. They establish the 'ethical superstructure' for every member of your team.

Ralph Waldo Emerson once said, "What lies behind you and what lies before you are tiny matters compared to what lies within you."

You must have values which are clearly set forth and communicated to your employees.

When a business has a strong ethical superstructure there is an inherent foundation in place to guide the actions of individuals when they are faced with making decisions.

I have often heard clients complain that, as their companies were growing, decisions that were delegated to subordinate managers were 'not made the way that I would have made them'.

This statement is symptomatic of the failure on the part of the leader to communicate a clear ethical superstructure.

The ethical superstructure must be explicitly understood by each member of your team.

When you force your team members to guess your values, you are expecting a miracle to occur.

THE PLEDGE

A few years ago I consulted with a national rental car agency which was trying to create and ingrain a strong level of commitment within its employees.

During our strategic planning retreat we explored a number of areas which the management team believed were important to the success of the business. One of the operational managers offered a commitment point which stated that 'we should honor every reservation commitment'.

The CFO of the company reacted very negatively to this proposal. He believed that a commitment to 'honor every reservation commitment' would put the company in serious financial jeopardy. A heated debate ensued and we agreed to re-examine this idea during the second day of the retreat.

The CFO brought the subject up on the following day. He offered that, after sleeping on it, he concurred with the original commitment point. As he put it, "If we can't honor every reservation commitment, we shouldn't be in this business."

Honor every commitment you make.

Your commitment statement points are critical messages that you create and send to your employees. They establish 'the pledge' that your team makes to every other person with whom they interact.

They are the driving forces which establish the way you would like your employees to treat their peers, their customers, their suppliers and their managers.

Commitment statements must be visceral.

Commitment statements empower your employees to treat other human beings the way you would treat them from a 'gut level'.

Commitment points must be emotionally and intellectually espoused by your team members.

PASSING THE TORCH

Develop five commitment points which most represent how you believe your business should be conducted.

COMMITMENT STATEMENT WORKSHEET

Our company is committed to:

1.

2.

3.

4.

5.

Communicate your commitments.

1. Meet with key managers to introduce the commitment statement and impress upon them the importance of maintaining these commitments in day to day operations.

2. Conduct meetings with each department to introduce the commitment statement.

3. Post the commitment statement in your office lobby and in visible areas throughout your facility.

4. Hire new employees who exhibit qualities which correspond to your commitment statement.

5. Hold your employees accountable for performing up to the standards set forth in the commitment statement.

Live your values.

SENSE OF PURPOSE

The word 'discipline' carries a heavy negative burden.

During our early years as infants and students the word 'discipline' was used to evoke control, obedience, enforcement and punishment.

Let's cast this often misunderstood tool in a different role.

Discipline is a means of developing self-control and efficiency.

It results from a positive environment which encourages you to perform to your best level of achievement while maintaining focus upon the interests of the organization.

Discipline creates a sense of purpose.

The proper application of discipline neither suppresses nor discourages individual originality or innovation. It facilitates creativity within an envelope of common objectives and pride in one's efforts.

Teach your team members the 'correct way' to do things.

Discipline provides the foundation for success in a world filled with options and hardships.

DETAILS, DETAILS...

Successful businesses exhibit a fanatical devotion to details.

Attention to detail should materialize in everything you do.

Are you providing the leadership to ensure that every activity of your team is being worked upon and completed as perfectly as possible?

How often do you hear someone say, "Well, no one is perfect?"

Is this an acceptable attitude within your team?

Would you want your auto mechanic to approach his work this way when he is working on your car's brakes?

Would you like an air traffic controller to have this perspective when you are about to land at Los Angeles International Airport?

Attention to detail requires consistent and constant performance.

It is no accident that McDonald's hamburgers taste and look the same whether you are in Boston, San Antonio or Singapore.

It is no coincidence that Motorola exacts the same high quality of product in Phoenix, Northbrook and Boynton Beach.

Examine the details of 'what matters' in your business.

Are you doing the best you can do in the:

- Preparation and review of contracts

- Design of products

- Follow up on sales leads and quotations

- Quality of workmanship in products

- Testing of products

- Training of employees

- Procedures for handling customer complaints

- Appearance of facilities

- Processing and payment of invoices

- Method in which the receptionist answers incoming telephone calls.

Emphasize the importance of the details that unsuccessful organizations take for granted.

SEVEN

**"Little progress has ever been achieved
without a plan."**

Unknown

CLUES YOU CAN USE

There are many definitions for strategic planning. The one I prefer came from a client in San Francisco.

Strategic planning is the creation of a blueprint for the future. It marries capabilities, market data, and dreams with available investment dollars.

Are you unsure of the value of strategic planning? If so, take this strategic planning test.

•Do you like the way things are?

•What is your "return on effort"? What is you "return on time"?

•Which decisions hurt your bottom line? Which ones help your bottom line?

•What is your core business?

•What pieces of your company make money? Which ones lose money? Are your answers based upon intuition or fact?

•Are you the low cost provider in your market? Do you know what low cost provider means? Can you quantify it?

•What decisions impact your cash position?

•Are you making and selling products and services that people want to buy?

•Do you ask your customers what they want to buy from you?

•Have you lost more customers in the past twelve months than you have gained?

Question everything you do - all of the time.

PUT ON YOUR SPACESUIT

In my youth I joined my schoolmates in our local gym to watch a small black and white TV project images of the first person in space, the first person to orbit the earth, the first...you name it, and NASA provided it to us. In those days, NASA was on a mission to put the first human being on the moon.

This enormous team shared a seemingly impossible vision. Spurred on by a promise made by President John Kennedy, NASA's array of technical and support people worked together over an extended period of time to achieve something only science fiction writers had dreamed before. It was truly a time to reach for the stars.

If you only do what you've always done, you'll achieve only what you've always achieved.

There is no reason why you can't have equally optimistic personal dreams, turn your dreams in plans, and turn your plans into reality.

Walt Disney is credited with saying, "If you can dream it, you can do it." His dreams in the 1950's have turned into a twelve billion dollar megaworld of entertainment, theme park, consumer product and resort operations in the mid-1990's.

How can you turn your dreams into reality?

•**Think big.** Your only limits are self-imposed.

•**Know what matters.** Shape your dreams around the important stuff.

•**Make your own luck.** Good luck occurs when opportunity meets someone who is well prepared.

•**Maintain your focus.** Wake up and end the day with the same dream.

•**Make plans.** Think it out and write it down.

•**Leap off the cliff.** Nothing starts until you do.

THE HEART OF THE MATTER

Some friends of mine own a neat little retail business in Honolulu. They constantly look for ways to improve their income and style of life. I admire their predisposition toward risk taking and the rate of success they have achieved with their customers when implementing new product and merchandising ideas.

One of their keys to success is knowing which questions to ask before they set out on a new course of action. Here is a key question you need to answer to grow your business and increase the satisfaction you derive from your daily efforts.

Why does your organization exist?

The most frequent answer to this question is 'to make a profit'. Let's try another answer.

Your organization exists solely because you are able to create, nurture and maintain customers.

The successful organization creates customers by understanding, and then providing, the products and levels of service which meet and exceed the customers' perceptions of value and quality.

Creating, nurturing and maintaining a customer requires that you satisfy a tangible need and provide constant reinforcement that the customer made the correct decision in choosing you as the provider.

Understand how your customers perceive value and quality.

To achieve this understanding you need to know how your customers perceive value and quality in the products and services they buy.

Here are some typical elements which constitute these perceptions of value and quality.

•A product or service which meets a specific need 100% of the time.

•100% on time delivery on a 'just in time' basis.

•A competitive price.

•A personal relationship with you, the supplier.

•A belief that you will stand behind your products and services.

Clearly understand the heart of 'what matters'.

"I LIKE THE WAY THINGS ARE"

If you catch yourself saying this you are headed for trouble.

We don't live in the Fifteenth Century with the luxury (or lack of opportunity) to settle into our current mode of living and stay there until we die. One of your charters as a manager is to endorse, or more accurately, espouse, the value and need for constructive change within your organization.

Sir Winston Churchill put it best when he said, "To improve is to change; to be perfect is to change often."

You may not be able to attain perfection but you must accept change as an inevitable and constructive force.

Look to the future as an opportunity to turn your dreams into profits.

Imagine that looking toward the future requires you to open a mysterious package called the Box of the Future. Your ability to utilize the future as an opportunity depends upon your perception of what is contained in this box.

Many managers see the Box of the Future as a Pandora's Box. They believe this Pandora's Box will present them with obstacles and hurdles which cannot be overcome. As a result these managers tend to turn a blind eye to the future and hope that 'things will work out'.

In order to best utilize all of your abilities, you must look at the Box of the Future as though it were a Christmas present neatly wrapped in decorative paper and ribbons. Open the Box of the Future with the optimistic anticipation experienced by children when they sit under the tree on Christmas morning.

Does the Box of the Future contain something you want? If not, does it contain an unanticipated surprise/obstacle/hurdle that you can use to your advantage?

Every obstacle presents an exponential number of opportunities for the future.

"I DON'T KNOW HOW"

Many managers who perceive the future in positive terms do so within some self-imposed constraints which limit creativity.

Analytical planners tend to turn planning into a mechanical process. The annual and 'strategic' planning functions in large corporations focus too narrowly upon a finished budgeting product. The emphasis upon charts, graphs and pro forma financial statements influences the way many managers view the future.

Analytical planners focus upon a fistful of numbers which foot and cross foot on a tidy spreadsheet.

Intuitive planners tend to 'wing it' by using half-truths and poorly researched assumptions as the basis for envisioning the future. The optimism of the intuitive planner is derived from an oversimplified, inductive understanding of industry half-truths.

Intuitive planners assume that increased sales will always equate to increased profits or maintaining high gross margin percentages is always better than attaining increased market share.

Intuitive planners focus upon doing more of the same.

How can you do it a better way? Use the Texas Four Step to examine the basic components of your business.

Establish the benchmark. The benchmark for strategic planning is utilized as the 'leaping off' point for the future. It helps you better understand such things as:

•What happened within and to your organization in the past?
•Where is your organization now?
•What decisions helped you or hurt you in arriving at the present?

The past is the prologue to the future.

THE FORM

Avid horse players and serious students of the sport of horse racing know "The Daily Racing Form" newspaper as the consummate source of information for wagering at off track betting establishments and race tracks across the country.

'The Form', as it is known to rail birds, provides in-depth coverage of the most recent past performances of all of the horses entered in each race on the daily racing card.

It shows each horse's post position, order of running at various poles, or milestones, during the race and the horse's position at the wire, or finish line.

'The Form' also contains comments on each horse's prior races in an effort to explain performance peculiarities such as 'bobbled at the start', 'boxed in at the turn', or 'lugged out in the stretch'.

When you review the past performance of your company you should create 'The Form' for each spike or downturn in your company's results.

If both sales and profits were up in 1991, why did this happen? If revenues increased and profits lagged in 1994, do you know why?

Be Honest with yourself.

1. Did your performance result from good luck or good decisions by you and your team members?

2. If there were extreme external factors, such as wars, taxes or landmark legislative actions, how did you respond?

3. How did your competition effect your performance?

In the early 1990's Operation Desert Shield/Desert Storm had a serious impact on the performance of Hawaiian Airlines. With Saddam Hussein threatening to terrorize international airports the luster of air travel to Hawaii evaporated. The airline's revenue per seat plunged.

Hawaiian Airlines saw this event as an opportunity rather than an excuse for poor performance,

By changing their short term goals and plans, the airline became one of the leading charter companies for transporting troops to the Middle East.

Learn from your mistakes and your successes.

SWOT TEAM

One of the few things you can believe with absolute certainty in this world is that each person and each group of people possesses a unique combination of strengths and weaknesses.

Those of you who are successful have found a way to capitalize upon your strengths and eliminate or diminish the importance of your weaknesses.

A former colleague of mine once provided consulting services to a highly successful food processing company in Florida.

He was constantly amazed at the ability of the company's management team to work through very difficult internal and external problems and maintain a record of increasing revenues and profits.

At the beginning of the consulting engagement, my friend asked the company's president for an explanation of the secret of the company's success.

"It's quite simple," replied the president, "we know our weaknesses, work them through and then eliminate them."

Know yourself.

One of the more effective techniques used in establishing the benchmark for strategic planning is what has come to be known as the SWOT analysis.

The SWOT analysis examines four key perspectives on the current position of the organization.

1. What are the company's **strengths** in terms of operations, products and services, business development, market share, relationships with customers and suppliers and overall image and reputation?

2. What are your current **weaknesses**? Weaknesses are current areas of deficiency which need to be addressed and resolved such as facilities which consistently lose money, ineffective products and services, inadequate development of managers and a poorly defined organizational structure.

3.   What **opportunities** do you have in the present and in the future? Look at new markets, additional geographical territories and new product development.

4.   What **threats** do you face? Threats tend to be contingent weaknesses which include natural disasters, litigation, and loss of key employees.

Be honest in your assessment.

Every weakness you identify provides an area for improving the productivity and profitability of your organization.

Your strategic plan should be created from the bottom up rather than from the top down.

It is critical to the eventual implementation of the plan that all of the people within your organization believe they play a major role in the creation of the future direction of the organization.

This presents a dilemma. If everyone in the organization is intimately involved in every step of the planning process your chances of accomplishing anything in a reasonable period of time are quite slim.

How do you include everyone and still create a timely plan for the future?

Let your employees know that you are initiating the strategic planning process. Tell them that their input is extremely important in creating the future for the company.

Send every employee a questionnaire. The ideas you receive from your mail room staff, your delivery drivers and your hourly production workers will surprise you.

Obtain input from your customers, your suppliers and even your bankers.

Ask the right questions.

Use the planning questionnaire worksheet as a guide.

PLANNING QUESTIONNAIRE WORKSHEET

1. What is your vision of the trends that will occur in your industry over the next three years?

2. What is your potential customer base and the types of products and services you should provide in the next three years.

3. What do your customers look for in the way of value and quality in your products and services?

4. What are the main strengths of your company?

5. What are the main weaknesses?

6. What are your key opportunities?

7. What threats are facing your company?

8. What change(s) would you make if you owned the company?

9. What should be done in the next twelve months to increase sales, gross margins, and operating profits?

Use a fresh environment to create fresh ideas.

Take your team members away from the office to develop your strategies for the future. Spend a weekend at the beach, in the mountains or out in the desert.

Set aside a portion of your time to do something together out in the fresh air. This will help you maintain a high level of energy.

In my high school days we studied a broad range of sciences which included an introduction to anatomy. Our textbook contained a really slick section of transparencies which displayed the human body.

When we looked at the first page of this section we saw the external, or epidermal, view of the human form. By turning the page we peeled back a layer to reveal the musculature system. Another page yielded the nervous system, then the internal organs, and, finally, the skeletal system.

As each page was turned we were able to examine the human body in a progression from the external, or obvious, to the internal, or specific functions.

Your strategic plan should be developed by 'peeling back the layers' in a similar manner.

Start with global ideas from your SWOT analysis.

Combine the lists of weaknesses, opportunities and threats. Utilize the input of your team members to prioritize this combined list.

Make a new list of the ten highest priority items. You have now peeled back one layer to create your 'Top Ten Hit List'.

Set a goal. Peel back another layer. Start working on the number one priority item on your hit list. Conduct a brainswarming session to determine what your team wants to achieve. Be specific.

Create a team-wide business improvement goal. Make it a quantifiable goal. Establish when you want to achieve your goal. Set dates.

Creat strategies. Peel back one more layer. What plans of attack can you develop to reach your goal? Make a list of potential strategies for your goal. Select one of these strategies.

Develop 'what, who and when'.

Now you're getting 'down to the bones'. Generate a list of action steps for your first strategy. Write them down using the format from your Meeting Minutes Worksheet.

Establish one team member to be responsible for achieving each action step. Negotiate an agreed upon completion date for each action step.

Monitor results. Determine how each activity will be measured and documented. Standardize your reporting methods so each team member and manager clearly understands how the team is progressing.

Success depends upon the choices you make today for tomorrow.

Return to your 'Top Ten Hit List'. Work priority item number two from your list through the same process beginning with the establishment of a goal.

When you have created the 'what, who and when' action steps for item two proceed on to the remaining items on the hit list.

Follow up.

Establish scheduled milestone meetings to follow up on the action steps. Incorporate the follow up into your ongoing "A" Team meetings.

EIGHT

**"Those of you who don't have goals
are used by those who do."**

Anonymous

BOWLING IN THE DARK

One of the advantages of working with numerous companies in a consulting capacity is the frequent number of opportunities to give presentations to professional organizations. This results in exposure to other professional speakers who usually have some insightful and beneficial things to say.

A few years ago I had the opportunity to speak at a convention in Honolulu which featured John Ueberroth, the COO and president of Hawaiian Airlines, as the keynote speaker.

The theme of his presentation was the utilization of goals in empowering your employees. Mr. Ueberroth told a story that went something like this:

"When I assumed the management of the airline I found that one very important element for success was lacking. There was no appreciation, or understanding, of the concept of goals. I was determined to illustrate this need in order to make the company successful."

"Imagine this. You go bowling with a group of friends. After renting your shoes and picking out a bowling ball, you stand at the end of the alley to roll your first frame. As you look down the lane you become aware that you cannot see the pins."

"You roll the ball down the alley into sheer darkness. As your ball returns you look up at the scoreboard. No score is posted. Another roll into darkness is followed by another blank on the scoreboard."

"How many games, or even frames, would you bowl before it dawned on you that this is the most boring thing you have ever done?"

Your team members need something to shoot for.

Create the environment for your team members to excel.

If you force your team to 'bowl in the dark' how can they be excited about coming to work?

They have no objectives and no feedback
on how they are doing.

You are condemning them to days filled with
seemingly unimportant tasks.

Give your employees the benefit of the doubt. Believe that they want to achieve something other than a paycheck.

Each member of your team needs a target to shoot for and public recognition for her or his level of performance.

Negotiate goals and post results.

Do you know how to hold your team members accountable for their performance?

Some managers think that ranting and raving about what they perceive to be failures on the part of their team members is an acceptable form of holding people accountable for their actions.

The inherent fault with this approach - not counting the leader's bad attitude - centers upon the absence of predetermined standards for what each team member is supposed to achieve.

Expectations become goals when they are negotiated and written down.

Those of you who have tried to master the sometimes mystical game of golf are aware that each hole on a golf course has an established standard of performance known as par.

Par determines the number of shots you are supposed to hit on a given golf hole, such as par three, par four or par five.

When you use five shots on a par four hole, you are aware that you did not reach your goal. In a similar fashion, a score of four on a par four hole represents a measure of solid achievement. A rare score of three on a par four hole indicates a certain quantifiable level of excellence for most golfers.

The establishment of par on a golf hole is a relatively simple technique which is usually determined by the length of the hole as stated in terms of yardage.

You have probably found that establishing par, or the acceptable level of performance for each of your team members, is a highly complex venture.

Negotiate acceptable levels of performance.

1. Determine what you believe each team member should achieve.

2. Ask your team members what they think they can achieve.

3. Negotiate each team member's 'par', or projected level of performance, in a team meeting.

    Use the group to inspire each team member to establish high individual standards.

    Utilize the team to hold each individual responsible for accomplishing his or her individual performance goal.

A COMPETITION OF IDEAS

Competition in the workplace is good stuff. The best sales organizations are fanatical about developing and posting goals and results in public places.

When sales team members have predetermined objectives they tend to achieve at a higher level than if they are just trying 'to do the best they can do'.

Goal setting and public recognition of personal and team achievements should not be limited to the sales function.

Competition should be used to enable individuals to focus upon their personal achievements as measured against their own benchmarks.

Your role as the manager and teacher of your team members will be fostered and expedited by implementing goals and follow up systems within your area of responsibility. Where do you start?

The first step is to understand that there are two categories of goals which need to be identified and addressed for each of your team members, In order to help them grow and reach beyond the limits of their capabilities, your team members need to focus upon both Personal Enrichment Goals and Business Improvement Goals.

What is the difference between these two types of goals?

Personal Enrichment Goals, or PEGs, are individual objectives which are established - negotiated - to allow each member of your team to focus upon areas of personal improvement in career-related functions. Personal Enrichment Goals typically concentrate on such disciplines as communicating, delegating, time management, decision making, team building and creating better personal relationships.

Business Improvement Goals, also called BIGs, are quantifiable, precise commitments for each individual. These goals are also negotiated. Business Improvement Goals focus upon each individual's area of responsibility and include production targets measurable quality enhancements, productivity, and cost savings

Every member of your team needs goals.

MOUNTAINEERING

Managing the growth of your staff is similar to coaching them in the art, or science, of indoor mountaineering.

Much like climbing a rock wall, your employees are constantly traversing through their careers...moving up one peg at a time...pausing to catch their balance at the new level...looking above them toward the next level of achievement...then stretching upward, reaching out toward a higher plateau of responsibility and expertise.

One of the tools you can use to facilitate the climb is the Personal Enrichment Goal system.

The Personal Enrichment Goal system is founded on the reality that, when a team is striving to achieve something, the ability to excel is dependent upon the extreme personal effort of every member of the team.

How do you achieve this 'extreme personal effort'?

1. **Develop Personal Enrichment Goals.** Meet with each one of your team members to establish personal management areas of improvement. Focus upon personal skills which enhance each team member's ability to work more effectively within the team.

2. **Establish action steps, time frames and milestones for achieving the goals.** Be specific. Determine what needs to be done. Establish reasonable completion dates and interim dates. Write them down.

3. **Follow up consistently.** Record the completion dates and interim dates on your calendar for each team member. Meet with each team member religiously to review progress and success.

4. **Let every team member know how important the Personal Enrichment Goal system is to them.** Coach, facilitate, lead the cheers, reinforce. Be the driving force behind the personal enrichment of each of your team members.

PERSONAL ENRICHMENT GOALS

You are the initiator and facilitator for the Personal Enrichment Goal program for each of your team members. It is up to you to teach them how to establish Personal Enrichment Goals and ensure that they clearly understand the importance of each of the goal elements.

How do you, and your team members, create these Personal Enrichment Goals?

1. **Focus on what matters.** Each team member has one or more personal management or business skills which could be improved upon. Assist each team member in identifying and accepting these areas for personal improvement.

2. **Mean It.** Personal Enrichment Goals must be accepted by each individual. One of the best methods I have found for developing ownership of a goal or commitment is a simple prefatory statement - "I will...!"

    When your team members understand that statements such as "I hope to...," "I would like to...," or "I'll try to..." are not acceptable expressions of commitment, you will make major strides in establishing individual accountability within your organization.

3. **Own it.** A Personal Enrichment Goal is just that - personal! Your team members must understand that it is totally their responsibility - not yours, their friends or anyone else's - to work on and achieve their own Personal Enrichment Goals. They need to be 120% focused upon success.

4. **Go for it.** Write it down. Establish a plan of attack.

    Create specific actions under the category of **What**.

    Set milestones and completion dates as targeted by **When**.

    Use the Goal Worksheet to record the goals.

THE MANAGER'S TOOLBOX
GOAL WORKSHEET

NAME: DATE: PERIOD:

GOAL:

WHAT   WHEN

1.

2.

3.

4.

5.

ACHIEVEMENT:

Team members must also stay focused on the BIG's.

The Business Improvement Goal system is one of the most important tools you will implement to generate individual and team-wide accountability. Business Improvement Goals force your team members to maintain their focus on the key bottom line activities of your organization.

The golden goal pyramid.

When each of your team members has goals which tie into the goals of the team, which in turn tie into the overall goals of the organization, you have created a pyramid for success. If each building block (or goal) is in place (or achieved) the pyramid will be built upon a solid foundation for lasting success.

How do you create this structure for success?

1. **Negotiate Business Improvement Goals based upon 'what matters'.** Business Improvement Goals should be negotiated in a group setting. Communicate the company goals. Review what your team needs to contribute to enable the organization to reach these goals.

   Break the team goals into individual pieces. Use the team to help determine who should be responsible for each piece.

   Negotiate the individual goals. The presence of the other team members will provide a certain degree of peer pressure to inspire each team member to set aggressive but attainable goals.

2. **Establish 'what and when' action steps for each goal.** Conduct a brainswarming session to capture the ideas of the team members to help create these action steps.

3. **Follow up.** Review the progress of each team member toward reaching the goals during your "A" Team meetings.

   Acknowledge performance. Use the entire team to help create solutions for a team member who is falling behind schedule.

THE BIG FORMULA

Abstract concepts are acceptable for mathematicians and scholars but not for the majority of people in your organization.

When you are able to simplify new ideas into concrete, easily understood applications your chances for success are magnified.

Packaging sells, but it also teaches.

How can you package the Business Improvement Goal system so that your team members will be able to incorporate it into the way they practice management and achievement on a day to day basis? Use this simple goal formula.

BIG GOAL FORMULA

GOAL STATEMENT

I will (Increase/Decrease/Attain) (What Matters)
by ($; %; Volume; Quality; Productivity)
by (Date).

PROFIT STATEMENT

As a result of achieving this goal,
I will (Earn/Save) ($)
in bottom line profit.

Use the Goal Worksheet to record your team members' goals.

Goals turn motion into action.

NINE

"Passionate team members are your strongest catalysts for change."

Anonymous

THE POWER OF PASSIONATE PEOPLE

My thoughts on passion in business have developed over a period of years working with successful people who feel strongly about what they are doing and what they want to achieve. They outperform their peers for a number of reasons, but the one common element of their success is their passion for what they are doing.

Passion, as defined in the New World Dictionary, means, among other things, a 'strong emotion' and 'enthusiasm'. A former client of mine gave a speech to a group of sales managers in which he discussed enthusiasm. "Enthusiasm," he said, "is best understood when you look at the last four letters in the word...IASM. These letters stand for I Am Sold Myself!"

If you, too, are 'sold yourself', your enthusiasm becomes contagious. Your passion will generate exponential gains in your team's performance.

In the 1957 movie "The Bridge on the River Kwai", Colonel Nicholls, played by Sir Alec Guiness, led his group of British World War II prisoners of war to complete the nearly impossible task of building a wooden train trestle across a river in Thailand surrounded by jungle.

While the construction of the bridge served the Japanese army's purpose of completing a railway link between Bangkok and Rangoon, Colonel Nicholls was less interested in the strategic significance of the undertaking than he was in the moral victory it provided for his troops and against his captors. "We are going to show these people," he said, "what men in the British army are capable of, even in the worst possible conditions."

Significant change arises when someone has the courage to stand up and passionately state her or his position and beliefs.

Passion in the workplace is essential for fostering positive change. In constructive work environments, creativity is best served by granting all of the participants an open forum for expressing their views.

MOTIVATION

I love to ask managers if they believe they can motivate others.

They almost always say, "Yes."

Then I ask them to consider another possibility. You can't motivate other people. They are already motivated. They do the things they do for their own, individual reasons, not yours.

Your job as a manager is to create an environment where people do things for their reasons which help obtain the results the organization wants to achieve.

This perception opens up a whole new understanding of motivation. Do you know managers who are supposed to be great motivators? Do you believe they can motivate people they don't know?

Bill Parcells, the former head football coach of the New York Giants, was asked about his abilities as a motivator during a televised interview on the eve of his second Super Bowl victory. Coach Parcells said, "I hate to use the word motivation. I try to instill an interest in the individual to make him pursue and utilize the information we provide him to meet the objectives of the organization."

Don Coryell, the former head coach of the San Diego Chargers, once said, "The country is full of good coaches. What it takes to win is a bunch of interested players."

How do you create
'a bunch of interested players'?

1.   Understand your team members. Get to know them. What are they trying to achieve in their lives?

2.   Make a list of your team members. Write down what you believe to be the most important things that motivate each one of them.

3.   Validate these key motivators for each team member through communication and other social and business interaction.

EVEN A BRICK WANTS TO BE SOMETHING

In the recent hit movie "Indecent Proposal" there is a scene in which Dave, the character played by Woody Harrelson, has returned to a teaching position at the collegiate level.

Dave, an accomplished professional architect, is presenting a slide show to a class of architectural underclassmen. After viewing several buildings constructed of brick and masonry he holds up a brick and says, "Even a brick wants to be something."

The 'bricks' that are the foundation of your organization are the people who show up every day to make personal contributions to the success of the business. And every one of these people wants to be something, or someone, too.

Do you underestimate the desires and the abilities of your workers? The people in your work force make important decisions in their personal lives everyday.

•They make commitments for leasing residences.

•They obtain mortgages for their homes.

•They finance or lease automobiles.

•They plan and save for their childrens' educations.

Your employees are going to 'be something' anyway; why not give them the opportunity to 'be something' at work?

Create an environment which allows your people to be something.

1. Keep them informed of the overall goals of the organization.

2. Allow them to develop their personal contributions to the overall goals.

3. Let them breathe the fine air of decision-making.

4. Tell them how their performance and decisions have benefited the organization.

TIME BEHIND THE WHEEL

I recently took the opportunity to enjoy something I have wanted to participate in for over twenty years - the intriguing world of auto racing. I originally enrolled in a racing school at the now defunct Riverside Raceway but, shortly before the class was to begin, I received an invitation to visit Hong Kong and the People's Republic of China as member of a business mission.

So it was with a great deal of anticipation that I finally joined my classmates in a three day racing class at the Russell Racing School at Laguna Seca Raceway.

The first day and a half was devoted to practicing some of the essential skills required to operate a race car - braking, shifting, down shifting and cornering. These exercises were accompanied by classroom instruction and a long, slow walk around the 2.2 mile track to familiarize ourselves with the nuances of the unique corners at Laguna Seca, including the famous Corkscrew.

Following lunch on the second day our instructors told us it was time to 'turn us loose for time behind the wheel'. They pointed out that the only way to learn how to drive a race car was to actually do it! We had been well prepared through our practice sessions and our instructors had no reservations about 'turning us loose' in the school's $20,000 Formula Ford race cars.

This experience made me think about business owners and managers who are reluctant to 'turn their employees loose' to make decisions and assume responsibilities.

Give your team members their 'time behind the wheel'.

1. Make sure that they understand what you, and they, are trying to achieve.

2. Train them well and thoroughly.

3. Put them to the 'acid test'. Create opportunities for success. Create opportunities for failure.

FREEDOM

Freedom, according to Miles Davis (and others), is intelligence.

Freedom, according to Janis Joplin (and others), is when you have nothing left to lose.

So what is freedom, anyway?

Freedom occurs when you can do anything you want to do, and what you want to do is something that will have a positive impact upon the people you touch everyday.

To be a successful manager you have to be free.

Your managers are not free if you:

•Unilaterally usurp their authority.

•Are abusive to them in private or in front of others.

•Veto their decisions without discussion.

•Set their budgets without their input.

•Make sales directly to their customers which they know nothing about.

•Give directions to their staff without their knowledge.

If you are guilty of any of the above, it's time to wake up.

FINDING PASSIONATE PEOPLE

One of the debacles of professional life is that most managers spend more time agonizing over firing current employees than they devote to the conscientious effort toward hiring new team members.

No matter how hardened you may believe you are in the termination process, letting an employee go is never a pleasant undertaking. The next time you are faced with terminating an employee, stop and review how much, or how little, time you spent when you hired that person. Did you truly seek the best person you could find, or did you take the path of least resistance?

You have to build your team with the best people you can find.

I look at it this way. In very round numbers, your time between the years of twenty and sixty is broken out as follows: one third of your time asleep, one third of your time in various forms of recreation and family obligations and one third of your time at work. Or, to put it more succinctly, you spend approximately one half of your waking hours during this period of your life involved in your work effort.

Don't surround yourself with a bunch of slugs.

Here are some traits you should look for in the group of people with whom you will be spending half of your waking hours.

1.   A positive outlook on life.

2.   A desire to achieve something more than a paycheck.

3.   An appreciation of her or his fellow worker.

4.   A warm sense of humor.

5.   One or more important interests outside of the workplace.

How do you find these people?

"WHAT AM I DOING HERE?"

A good place to start is a comprehensive job description. What, specifically, is the job applicant going to be responsible for?

The job description should include a combination of both technical and managerial tasks that are clearly set forth in terms and words that are understandable for the candidate at the appropriate position level.

Think it through.

Too many job descriptions are written for the benefit of the management team and the human resources department rather than for the employee.

You can't expect employees to guess or understand through some form of mystical osmosis exactly what you want them to do each day. If you take this approach, the odds of any given employee successfully guessing what you want him or her to do is approximately that same as accurately predicting the complete finishing order of the next Kentucky Derby.

Give each employee the best opportunity to be successful.

In addition to setting forth the technical and managerial responsibilities for each position, be sure to focus upon the required interaction with other employees and departments.

The necessity for effective communication and understanding with others is often overlooked in defining jobs.

Prospective employees are frequently left with the impression that, in order to be successful, they are going to be working in a void. Emphasize the organization's belief in teamwork.

Be specific regarding which groups of people must be involved in the candidates success. By doing this you foster the teamwork necessary for the new employee, and the organization, to achieve the objectives that result in success.

GREAT EXPECTATIONS

A critical step in the hiring process for a new team member is the establishment of performance criteria.

If you were applying for a job, how comfortable would you be if your prospective employer was unable, or unwilling, to clearly identify the key, measurable elements of your potential success or failure?

How will success be evaluated?

New employees (or current ones, for that matter) should not be placed in situations where they are required to guess whether or not they are meeting your performance expectations. When forced to guess how their performance is being reviewed by management, employees tend to become indecisive, suspicious and self-serving. The net result is deleterious to the individual, the team, the overall working environment and the productivity of the organization.

Performance criteria should be written down clearly and precisely and contain measurable and reportable elements. It should incorporate both Business Improvement Goals and Personal Enrichment Goals, and include milestones and a completion date for each goal. Once an employee has been hired, these specific performance targets should be fleshed out by creating action steps to achieve the objectives.

Passionate employees need career paths.

In addition to the basic elements of performance criteria, each candidate needs to understand what it will take to move on to the next and subsequent position levels. The checklist for creating a career path should include:

1. Performance criteria for advancement.

2. A progression of satisfactory and improving performance reviews. The performance review instrument should be presented to each job applicant and discussed during the hiring process.

3. A schedule of technical and management development training.

PROFILING

One of the steps in the hiring process that is frequently overlooked is the definition of the personal traits you are looking for in a new team member.

It is one thing to define the job, and a further advancement to create the performance criteria, but how many of you think through the type of individual who will best fit in your organization?

It is important for the management team, as well as the working team members, to take the time to come to agreement upon the unique personal and technical skills required to function in a specific position.

Another critical consideration is the role the new team member will play in her or his interaction with the other team members.

What personal characteristics are needed to best contribute to the overall group effort? Remember, recruiting a team member is like preparing a gourmet meal. If one part of the recipe doesn't fit, the chemistry of the entire team is jeopardized.

Create the profile for your successful job candidate.

The basic tool for profiling is called the Must Have/Want analysis.

The 'Must Have' category includes those characteristics and skills that a candidate has to have in order to be considered for a position.

The 'Want' category contains additional skills and traits that would be pluses, but not necessities, for the successful job applicant.

Create a list of elements to be considered. Some items are common to most profiling lists.

- Education.

- Technical certifications.

- Years of experience.

- Industry experience.

- Management experience.

- Personal skills, such as communicating and computer skills.

- Managerial skills, such as planning and business development.

- Commuting distance to work.

The next step is to brainswarm these elements and create a two column worksheet containing both the 'Must Have' and 'Want' skills and characteristics.

It is important to remember that the profiling team must be objective and avoid creating the profile with a particular candidate in mind.

PROFILING WORKSHEET

Here is an example of a Must Have/Want analysis for a controller for a mid-sized manufacturer in the electronics industry.

MUST HAVE	WANT
•Bachelors degree in business, major in accounting	•Masters degree in business or accounting
•No specified certification	•CPA certification
•At least eight years accounting experience with a manufacturing company	•Controller with a manufacturer
•At least three years experience as an assistant controller or senior accountant	•Electronics industry experience
•Communication skills	•Corporate tax expertise
•Strategic planning/budgeting capabilities	•MIS management

Turn profiles into recruiting tools.

An additional benefit of this profiling technique is the capability to easily convert the worksheet into an advertisement for publication. Here is an example using the above profile:

"An electronics manufacturer in Orange County, California seeks a controller with a bachelors degree - major in accounting; at least eight years of accounting experience with a manufacturing company, with three or more years at the senior accountant level or above; and strong planning and budgeting skills. The ideal candidate will be a CPA with corporate controller, MIS management and corporate tax experience in the electronics industry."

A NEEDLE IN A HAYSTACK

How do you find the single best job candidate?

If you are managing a poorly run company with little or no employee career advancement opportunities, no involvement by the work force in the decision making process, poorly thought out marketing programs and product lines, lower than market pay scales and limited visibility in the community, the best thing you can count on is good luck.   You are going to need it!

Here are some things to think about, and capitalize upon, in your expedition for discovering passionate people.

1.   **Deserve the best.** Great companies attract great people. If your company has the reputation as a good place to work, you will be barraged by an endless stream of resumes and successful, vibrant people appearing in your lobby looking for an opportunity to work for you.

2.   **Get out the word.** The number one source of new technical and managerial talent is word of mouth. If your employees like working for you, they will tell everyone they come in contact with about their great company.

3.   **Publicize your needs.** Use every available form of positive publicity to promote your position as a good employer. Generate press releases for trade publications to announce your new products. Write articles for your local newspaper to promote pride in your company.

4.   **Post job openings.** You never know what might happen when you post your open positions in prominent places throughout your facilities. Employees who have been overlooked will present themselves, and their potentially undiscovered talents, for your evaluation. Even if they do not turn out to be qualified for the job at hand, posting will provide a great opportunity for career planning.

5.   **Talk to your friends.** The more people know about what you are trying to achieve, the more good people you will attract.

"HI, I'M MIKE WALLACE"

Most of you look upon the task of interviewing job applicants as one part art, one part science and one part complete agony. With the fear of federal and state labor laws staring you squarely in the face, the tendency is to ask safe, meaningless questions which in turn elicit safe and equally meaningless responses.

How can you get the most out of these interviews?

You should realize that a resume is not the end definition of an applicant; it represents the initial prerequisite that allowed the applicant in the front door. Once you are facing the candidate it is counterproductive to ask for a regurgitation of the information which has been previously scrutinized by your human resources staff and you.

The applicant has to earn the job.

The applicant should earn the job based upon his or her responses today, not based on the resume of past performance. If you know how to ask the right questions you will enable, or coerce, the potential employee to prove to you that he or she deserves to work for your organization.

Here are some thoughts on interviewing that should take the anxiety out the interview process.

1.   Ask questions about applicants' real life experiences which have had nothing to do with their work.

2.   Let the applicant do most of the talking. Use the probing techniques that sales professionals utilize when determining needs in a potential customer. Most interviewers talk too much and listen too little.

3.   Provide three narrative questions in advance for the applicant to prepare responses for prior to the interview. During the interview, ask questions which are basically the same as the original questions, but from a different perspective. See how the applicant responds to this shift.

4.   Probe for past behavior vs. prior accomplishments.

TESTING

When I was in the electronics industry our company was constantly searching for new electrical and mechanical engineers.

One of the problems in evaluating resumes from engineering applicants is the difficulty in comparing educational equivalencies among university systems and work experiences throughout the world. We were never sure if engineers from particular European, Asian or American schools or companies had received similar technical training and experience.

We discovered that the best way to cut through the academic and work experience unknowns was to create our own, company specific technical tests which centered upon engineering applications that were required to make our products competitive.

Simulate the work requirements.

Every job applicant, from clerk to executive, should be given, and feel challenged by, a test for technical and managerial proficiency.

I have seen as many accounting managers hired who were unable to create balanced journal entries as I have seen produce delivery drivers who were unable to count. And please, if you are hiring a salesperson, make him or her sell something to you before you make the job offer.

You will probably find that a test containing four to six complex problems will be sufficiently challenging for advanced technical applicants and managers. At the very least, all applicants should be tested for basic reading and mathematical skills.

Predict behavior.

Another valuable form of information about your prospective employees comes from behavioral tests. There are a number of tests available which provide remarkably accurate insights into the ways in which individuals will respond to challenges, procedures and the pace of your environment.

TEN

**"When the sun comes up, the lion
knows he has to outrun the slowest gazelle...**

**When the sun comes up, the gazelle
knows he has to outrun the fastest lion."**

From an African story

THE PIG IN THE PYTHON

My father used to assist the officials at the St. Louis Zoo when it was feeding time for the zoo's largest captive python. Pythons are known for gorging themselves on large animals during their infrequent meals.

He loved to tell the story of how fifteen men would stretch the python out and hold it down while an animal keeper would shove a pig down the python's thoat with a battering ram. The python would then go into a dormant stage while the lump that used to be a pig slowly worked its way through the reptile's digestive system.

A large contract or a huge project can have the same debilitating effect upon your organization if you swallow more than you can handle.

All of the other areas 'that matter' seem to grind to a halt while your team members focus upon the 'pig' as it works its way way through the system.

Don't let one large project put the rest of your organization 'out of control'.

Review your opportunities. Will the pursuit of any of them throttle the rest of your organization?

Maintaining control of your team or organization requires an honest appraisal of your true capabilities.

You must make a distinction between pursuing constructive opportunities and blindly accepting challenges that far exceed your present resources.

Don't bite off more than you can chew.

Don't chew more than you bite off.

SIDE OUT

When I lived near Washington, DC in the late 1970's I spent many Sunday afternoons playing pickup volleyball games along the Potomac River near the Lincoln Monument. Team captains were selected randomly to choose the sides for each game.

Some captains would negotiate with other captains to build teams that were comprised of fewer players with greater skills than their opponents. "Tell you what," he or she would say, "I'll take these six and play the other eight of you."

This 'noble' offer was predicated upon a selfish desire to win the game. It also represented a basic principal of sound team management.

Be one person light.

Your team should be designed to function with at least one less person than you think you need. This will keep you focused upon hiring the best people you can hire, people who will consistently perform at no less than a 120% or better level of effort.

Imagine that your team is a single block of stone. Place an explosive under this block and blow it up. Isolate each function. Start with a blank sheet of paper to reallocate each of these activities.

Some things to look for:

1. Has your team become overly specialized?

2. Do some team members fill up their schedules with activities because they have nothing else to do to with their time?

3. Are the functions your team members perform best matched up with their individual skills?

4. If you were to eliminate one person from your team would the things they are responsible for still get done? Would they get done better?

Do more with less.

THROUGH THE STORM

It has been said that adversity brings out the best in the best of us. It is relatively simple for a manager to lead a team in a nearly perfect world where there is an abundant source of talent, physical resources and customers.

Have you ever experienced such a perfect world? If so, lucky you. If not, you know the challenges that a leader is faced with almost every day.

A leader achieves goals in the absence of unlimited resources.

The captain of a ship finds it somewhat easy to steer the ship on course in the best of conditions. But what happens when there is rough weather?

In the face of a tropical storm, the true leader is able to keep the ship on course through the surging seas and still maintain the ship's direction toward the eventual destination. Any effort less than this only requires the skills of a pilot.

Pilots steer tugboats; Leaders guide ships.

In my early twenties I went through what I affectionately look back upon as my 'outward bound' years. I was, in no particular order, a truck driver, carpenter, tower crane operator and civil engineer on various construction sites.

One project I worked on was destined from the beginning to be a disaster. After a number of false starts the absentee developer hired an experienced superintendent to take over the job and salvage what was left of the potential profits. Jack Herky was a leader.

He took over a project which was months behind schedule filled with 'morale buster' employees and literally stuck in the red clay mud. Jack knew what it would take to get this operation on track. And he succeeded!

Leaders maintain the vision - no matter what.

"ROLLOVER, HUXLEY"

One day I returned home from work to find an odd looking dog sitting on my front door step. This dog, a dirty, street worn mixture of poodle and some other unknown breed, was obviously on the run, hungry and looking for a new place to live.

I named my new friend Huxley, after Aldous, of course, and took him into my apartment as a roommate. The only skills which Huxley possessed were begging at the dining room table and - during evening walks - the ability to scour through the local garbage dumpster and emerge with a discarded piece of toast.

Huxley became a challenge to me. Could this old worldly dog learn new tricks? Every night I tried to teach this guy something new. He wasn't very good at sitting up or shaking hands, but, for some reason, Huxley took to the 'rolling over' routine.

A success in the face of canine apathy!

The best leaders are always learning something new.

If you think you know everything you are in huge trouble. In my travels through life I have never met anyone of any real substance who didn't want to learn something new every day.

Are you still learning something new every day? Is each member of your team learning something new every day? Is your management style preventing you or any of your team members from learning something new every day?

Create a learning environment.

1.   No one on your team should ask all of the questions, including you.

2.   No one on your team should have all of the answers, including you.

3.   Every member on your team should be able to question what the team is doing, and why.

GO AT IT WITH BOTH HANDS

People who are able to achieve results of significance are whirlwinds of activity. They always seem to be doing something, to be learning something, to be interested in something.

Where do they get the energy to 'keep at it'?

Passion is a word which is usually associated with physical human activities. People who kill those they love or hate do so in 'crimes of passion'. We make love with a new lover with 'passionate desire'. We read books about 'passionate love triangles'.

Passion is rarely connected with the concept of motivation in the office or workplace. But, if you want to be truly successful at what you are doing, you need be passionate about it, consumed by it, and ready to 'go at it with both hands'.

It has often been said that Jack Nicklaus is the greatest professional golfer of all time. He supposedly keeps himself on track by remaining 'enthusiastically dissatisfied'.

What a great outlook for success! Be enthusiastic and always try to do better than you are doing at the present moment.

Provide the adrenalin for your team.

As the leader of your team you need to be the one who provides the inspiration and energy to keep your team members excited about what they are doing.

Share your dreams and your goals with your team. Keep them intoxicated with the desire to perform and continually foster the fervency and drive which breeds individual and group success.

The team assumes the character of the leader.

If you aren't excited about what you and your team are trying to achieve, you can be sure that your team members will approach their responsibilities with nonchalance and inertia.

The expression of 'lead or get out of the way' applies to you!

THE EYE OF THE POET

Those of us who teach, consult and write for a living are constantly aware of the need to be sensitive to the perceptions of the people with whom we communicate and interact on a daily basis.

If you can't envision ideas, problems and solutions from the perspective of other managers and team members, how can you expect to be effective in your relationships with them?

When you learn how to see the world as others see it and are able to intellectually adopt their outlook on various subjects and positions, you may then attain that unlimited degree of emotional freedom which allows you to best understand and inspire other human beings.

Feel the world from other perspectives.

In order to understand the viewpoint of other people, you need to first come to terms with yourself. It's been said that if someone could buy you for what you're worth and sell you for what you think you're worth, a tidy profit could be made.

Are you realistic and honest with yourself about the value you provide to your organization? A friend of mine once told me, "If I only had a little humility, I'd be perfect." Could you use 'a little humility', too?

Think about the people who helped you when you were trying to learn and develop your management skills. Were they effective at seeing the world through your eyes?

Reach back and help the people behind you.

1. Take stock of the members of your team. Try to understand what they want to achieve in their careers.

2. Now take another step closer to your team members. Where did they come from? What are their needs for their families?

3. Help your team members channel their needs into constructive efforts for them, their families and your organization.

PIANO LESSONS

A friend of mine once characterized her company's management team in terms of playing the piano.

The managers who were organized, prepared and confident were described as 'playing the piano with both hands and feet'. Those managers who were tentative and closed minded were depicted as 'playing one key at a time and just thumping away'.

How do you play the piano?

Prepare yourself, then pull the trigger.

Lord Lawrence Olivier, the late star of British stage and international cinema, is attributed with saying, "To be a great actor, one needs the humility to prepare and the self-confidence to bring it off."

Monica, my neighbors' seven year old daughter, had been taking piano lessons for eight months. On the night of her first piano recital she walked out on stage in a beautiful new dress in front of a huge - maybe thirty people - audience and promptly froze up.

Little Monica was certain that the world would come to an end because of her monumental failure. To her surprise Monica's parents still loved her, her brother still appreciated her and her friends - although they snickered a little bit - were still her friends.

Six months later Monica faced the challenge of her second recital with a confident and artistic performance. She had attained a new level of confidence by overcoming her fear of failure.

Woody Allen is quoted as saying, "80% of success is just showing up." Those of you who continue to 'show up' learn that participation brings both success and failure.

Confidence arises when you are free from the fear of failure.

HEROES AND ZEROS

Have you ever worked for a patently dishonest person?

In the early years of my career, I knew an executive named Ted who was incredibly successful when measured by short-term image and monetary standards. Ted had skyrocketed onto the business scene in a sales capacity and leaped into a management position while he was still in his early thirties.

Ted's meteoric rise was followed by an equally catastrophic fall because he had one overriding flaw - Ted couldn't tell the truth.

The organization takes on the values of the leader.

Unfortunately, Ted's dishonesty became the pervasive method for doing business within his team. Ted - and his team members - lied to customers, vendors, peers, other team members and, eventually, the corporate officers and board members.

The twisting of truths worked to his team's advantage during Ted's early years with the company, but eventually even those people who had once revered his performance found his self serving approach to be inconsistent with the goals of the organization.

When Ted corkscrewed into the ground, his team went with him.

Say what you mean and do what you say.

I used to spend hours meeting with an eighty year old gentleman named Louie who had co-founded his company when he was twenty-eight years old. At the time of our meetings, he was still functioning as the president of his seafood curing and packing company.

Louie attributed his success and longevity in the business to one basic principle - do nothing which, after being done, leads you to tell a lie.

Your handshake and your word bind your actions.

SAM THE SLAM

Sammy owned and personally managed a regional automotive parts distribution company. He believed that the sole purpose of his employees was to perform tasks, pick up their paychecks and go home.

When members of Sam's management team brought up the need for the employees to enjoy their work, his response was, "They're not supposed to have fun here, they're supposed to work!"

Shouldn't work be fun? You spend about one half of your waking hours at your job. Do you want to condemn yourself, and those around you, to using fifty percent of your conscious lifetimes toiling in drudgery?

Lighten up!

Tom Landry was the head football coach of the Dallas Cowboys for over twenty years. He was known as the ultimate poker face among his peers.

A former player was once asked if he ever saw Coach Landry smile. "No, I didn't", he replied, "but remember, I only played there for five years."

A sense of humor and the ability to laugh at yourself are two of the healthiest characteristics you can obtain.

Put a bounce in your step.

1. Take those around you much more seriously than you take yourself.

2. Don't be a pessimist. Remember, a pessimist is someone who loans you money and doesn't expect to be repaid.

3. You are what you think about. Think about positive things.

RABBIT TRAILS

You may find from time to time that your organization seems to be wandering about with no real direction.

Does your team appear to be on no true course, with no objectives, and constantly finding the path of least resistance?

Rabbits tend to find small holes in the brush to make paths where there is nothing in their way. If you take the path of least resistance, you are probably heading to no true destination.

Maintain your focus.

One of the ways you can lose your focus is to rely upon reorganization as an essential method for improving your business.

"We trained hard, but it seemed that every time we were beginning to form into teams, we would be reorganized."

"We tend to meet any new situation by reorganization, and what a wonderful method it can be for creating the illusion of progress while producing mass confusion, inefficiency and demoralization."

This perspective was written - not in the 1990's - but rather 2,200 years ago by Petronius Arbiter, an officer in the Greek Navy.

If you find that you are using the reorganization process in an attempt to address your organization's shortcomings, you may be ignoring the real cause of your problems - lack of focus.

Do your team members know 'what matters'?

Do you constantly reinforce the goals and direction of your team?

Focus is the ability to think of one thing absolutely and absolutely nothing else.

ROUND PEGS IN ROUND HOLES

When I was a kid there was an advertiser on local New York City television shows named Lava Soap.

This product was promoted as the original super cleanser. It could clean any spot off of any material at any time.

Avoid the Lava Solution.

One of the critical mistakes you can make when you assume the leadership of a new company, division or department is to clean house before you create a new work environment.

Don't judge your new team members by the way they performed under someone else's direction.

Establish your atmosphere, complete with an emphasis on the values you believe in, and give your inherited staff the opportunity to perform for you.

Some of your team members will 'grab the bit' and run. Some of them will slink off into the shadows. Once you change the environment you can judge each team member's capacity for individual and group achievement.

Create an environment for good judgment.

Good judgment results when you have the right people in the right place at the right time with the right intentions and the right understanding of the values of the organization.

1.   Hire people with good intentions.

2.   Train your team members how to do things correctly.

3.   Give them the necessary tools.

4.   Remove the obstacles.

5.   Get out of their way!

THE BROOKLYN BRIDGE

In 1883 the Brooklyn Bridge was opened across 3,579 feet of the East River between the boroughs of Manhattan and Brooklyn. This new bridge became an immediate success for the transportation of commerce from Long Island to the bright lights of downtown New York City,

In 1964 another bridge was constructed in the Metropolitan New York area. This structure, the Verrazano-Narrows Bridge, spans 6,690 feet across the mouth of New York City's harbor between the boroughs of Staten Island and Brooklyn.

The span of the Brooklyn Bridge is equal to the task it was built to achieve, but this bridge would be a monumental failure if it had to reach across an expanse of nearly 6,700 feet.

Does your span of control make you feel like the Brooklyn Bridge trying to breach the entrance to New York's harbor?   In other words, are you trying to manage nearly twice the number of people you are capable of managing effectively?

Control your span of control.

Your span of control (defined) is the number of people who report directly to you.   There is no such thing as a 'textbook' span of control. In business school we were taught that the optimal span of control ranged between four and eight direct reports.   Is this the right solution for you?

If your managers are responsible for vastly different functions you should have a very tight, or small, span of control.   If the members of your team are performing very similar tasks you can manage a much larger span of control.

Are you running in too many directions at once?

Give yourself a span of control checkup.

Your span of control is determined by the diversity of functions performed by your direct reports.

PACKERS

Vince Lombardi, the former head coach of the Green Bay Packer football team, is famous for a number of accomplishments and quotations. One of his greatest achievements occurred during his first year at Green Bay, long before the world championships and Super Bowl victories.

When Coach Lombardi assumed his new responsibilities with the Packers he inherited a team which not only lost football games but had, unfortunately, become accustomed to losing.

The first task he undertook was to create a new way of doing things and a new group attitude geared toward success. He created a new agenda and sold this agenda to his team.

Your team must share your agenda.

The success of your agenda depends upon a 'gut level' acceptance by your team.

I frequently encounter new managers from the technical and operational ranks who think 'selling' is a dirty word.

In addition to 'mongering', 'hawking' and 'horse-trading', the definition of selling also includes such warm connotations as 'promoting', 'sharing' and 'publicizing'.

Shouldn't you promote, share and publicize your agenda?

1.   Develop a clear understanding of the benefits of your agenda.

2.   Utilize your team to create a plan for achieving your agenda. This will turn your agenda into their agenda.

3.   Celebrate your team's successes. Have spontaneous pizza parties, afternoons off, trips to local sporting events and concerts - and don't forget public pats on the back.

Practice the salesmanship of leadership.

BUNGEE JUMPING

One of the most exhilarating experiences in life is meeting up with another person who takes risks which are far beyond your scope of adventure.

You may think of yourself as a risk taker. Are you willing to risk your life, or your fortune, the way that a Formula One race car driver, a Banzai Pipeline surfer or an Australian bungee jumper does in a routine manner? Probably not. And maybe you shouldn't go to such extremes.

A colleague of mine once said, "Living at risk is like diving off a cliff and looking for water on the way down." When should you take drastic risks?

There is an often repeated story about a business owner who came up short of cash one week and was unable to cover the company's payroll.

He took a flight to Las Vegas, bet everything he had on one spin of the roulette wheel, doubled his money, went home, met payroll and wound up managing a successful international company.

While this may be a dramatized story, the point is that if great risks are required, the true leader understands this and behaves accordingly.

The risks you don't take don't produce anything.

The role of the leader in assuming risks and selling the team on taking these risks is evidenced by a strategy which has been used in wartime since humans first began confronting each other in religious and territorial disputes.

Historically, when an army was captured by the enemy, the captured army's leader was executed in full view of his troops. The loss of the key decision maker and risk taker usually obliterated the hopes and morale of the remaining prisoners of war.

Your team depends upon you to take successful risks.

ELEVEN

"Water maintains no constant shape."

from the ancient Chinese philosophers

OLD RED TOP

Derek Williams was known to most of his employees - behind his back, of course - as Old Red Top.

He was given this moniker by a dissatisfied management team member in recognition of Derek's predilection for becoming so angry at his employees that his face would turn a bright purplish-red as he stormed around the offices and across the manufacturing floor.

Derek tried to personally control every aspect of his business. He hired every employee, signed every check, authorized every purchase order and fired every employee whom he thought should be terminated.

Old Red Top's desire to control everything in his path left him with one very important part of his business which he could not control - himself.

Lack of control commands fear, not respect.

Fear should be looked upon as an unfortunate result rather than a realistic strategy for managing other human beings.

How can you ensure that you are able to maintain control of your own actions and reactions in your work environment?

1. Don't try to do everything yourself.

2. No matter how hard you try you will never be able to control every aspect of your life. As a mortician once said, "The size of your funeral will be determined by the weather."

4. Take a break from your work environment during the day. Go out for lunch. Take a ten minute walk out in the open air for your afternoon break.

5. Learn how to enjoy laughing at yourself.

Control yourself before you try to control your business.

THE DOCTOR'S OFFICE

You wake up early one morning to find that you are running a fever, your throat glands are swollen and your eyes and nose are itching and heavy. After canceling your appointments for the day you head off to visit your family doctor.

You are shown to an examination room by a nurse to undergo a series of basic tests - height and weight measurements, body temperature and blood pressure. Why are these tests performed?

Your doctor needs to have a clear understanding of your vital signs in order to to begin his or her diagnosis of your health. Your vital signs are then compared to standards - 98.6 degree body temperature, for example - to see how your body is functioning.

As a manager you must understand the vital signs of your organization in order to diagnose the condition and well being of your overall operation and team members.

Take the pulse of your team.

One of your responsibilities as a manager is to keep your finger on the pulse of your organization in a thorough and efficient manner. How do you achieve this?

1. Determine what is important. Know which areas of your responsibility are the most demonstrative of how effectively your team is operating.

2. Create the vital signs. You should concentrate on finding three to five things to measure which will give you a solid representation of how well you are doing.

3. Establish efficient methods for gathering the information on what is important. Collect this information without making the collection of the data become more important than the work which is being measured.

4. Gather the vital sign information consistently and thoroughly. Don't let sloppy data collection diminish the importance or integrity of the reported results.

YOUR FINGER ON THE PULSE

Take a step back, breathe deeply and look at your business as though you are a highly interested third party. What information do you need to determine how well your team is performing? What is the simplest way to obtain this information?

Understand the indicators
for your vital signs.

Organize your performance information into three categories. These categories supply data on your vital signs. Determine levels of performance which represent a very healthy condition, a stable condition and a critical condition for each part of your operation.

1.   Healthy condition. What parameters need to be met to indicate that your team is functioning well beyond the expected level of performance?

2.   Stable condition. This category represents solid achievement which is at or near the goals established for each function.

3.   Critical condition. The operations which fall into this category indicate trouble areas. Give these functions the highest level of visibility and fix the problems.

Tap all of your sources.

There are three methods of gathering information for determining your team's performance. These methods, called sources, are your financial results, your operating results and your personal relationships.

1.   Financial results come from your profit and loss statement and your balance sheet. Financial results include the supporting spreadsheets and other secondary records which are used to create your profit and loss statement and balance sheet.

2.   Operating results are performance reports which are created outside of the accounting and financial records. Operating results include employee turnover, productivity reports and safety performance.

3.   Personal relationships provide a more subjective look at the performance of your team. Personal relationships give you valuable feedback on customer satisfaction, supplier perspectives and the perceptions of your experienced line managers.

Use a combination of sources to determine your performance.

PSEUDO CERTAINTIES

The best and brightest products of our business schools often inhabit offices in near proximity to CEO's, CFO's and other high level corporate officers.

They come to the business arena armed with financial acumen, computer models and other forms of conceptual wizardry.

What kind of solutions do they bring to the game?

- •Have they built your product?

- •Have they turned in a billable hour?

- •Have they met face to face with your smallest customer?

If you hire highly credentialed graduates, the best thing you can do for them, and for you, is to 'dirty their hands' with the essence of your operations.

Give them the opportunity to learn 'what matters' to your business from the inside out and to gain the respect of your line managers who have helped you build your company.

Don't supersede your common senses.

We seem to be increasingly engrossed with numbers. We let our appetite for quantifying everything supplant our common sense.

Numbers and statistics provide you with some meaningful barometers but, as a colleague of mine said, "Statistics are like bikinis. What they reveal is far less interesting than what they conceal."

Your control mechanisms must allow you to capture 'what matters'.

Follow the 'sleep at night' principle.

1.   Which vital signs do you need to keep under control?

2.   What do you need to know to take the pulse of your organization?

3.   Set parameters around the important measurable activities.

4.   If the performance falls outside of these limits, you have a problem.

5.   If the results are within the parameters, you can enjoy a comfortable nights' sleep.

Conflicts between individual managers and team members are part of the landscape.

Healthy competition fosters excitement. It inspires heightened levels of activity and performance. Antagonism breeds disharmony. It infects your entire organization. The pervasiveness of hostile conflict reaches everyone in subtle and overt ways.

The analogy of the 'tangled net' derives from the Hawaiian philosophy that all things are related. The basis of the 'tangled net' is the understanding that disputes between family members effect every member of the family. Since the family is comprised of a 'net' of relationships, conflict between two or more participants within this net will cause discord within the entire group.

The Hawaiian culture contains a problem solving system for settling differences between family members. This system is known as *'Ho'oponopono'*, or 'setting to right'.

'Setting to right'.

Ho'oponopono is a highly complex system which is facilitated by third party healers. The basic process, however, involves four separate steps which are applicable to resolving disputes between team members in any environment.

1.   The opening. The symptoms of the problem are explored and peeled back to discover the root cause of the dispute.

2.   The discussion. All members of the 'net', or team, are asked to speak openly about their feelings surrounding the conflict and how the quarrel has affected them. They are also required to listen to each other.

3.   The resolution. The participants in the dispute must come to terms, settle their differences and grant forgiveness to each other.

4.   The closing. The results of the team meeting are summarized. The bonds that tie the team together are acknowledged and reaffirmed. The team members agree that the conflict will never again be discussed.

WHAT GETS MEASURED GETS DONE

Your team members will devote most of their attention to the things that are important to you. It is your responsibility to make sure they know what is important to you.

A manufacturing company posts the number of accident-free days in visible locations throughout the shop floor.

An accounting department 'awards' a cactus plant to the employee who makes the biggest blunder during the preceding month. The cactus must sit on that person's desk during the ensuing month.

A sales organization posts the daily and month-to-date performance of every sales person on a wall.

A trucking company 'awards' a pair of crutches to the general manager of each location which has an accident during the prior month. These crutches must be prominently displayed - upon the manager's office door! - for the following month.

What gets done gets recognized.

Develop creative methods for letting your team members know what is important to you.

1.   Publicize 'what matters'.

2.   Make the rewards and 'awards' significant, visible - and fun!

3.   Follow up consistently with your reward and 'award' programs.

4.   Keep thinking of new ways to emphasize 'what matters'.

5.   Enjoy the benefits of your efforts.

What gets recognized today gets done better tomorrow.

GOLD STARS

Many managers only communicate about the negative things that happen.

Your team members should look forward to their discussions and other interactions with you. It is important for them to believe that they will be recognized for their accomplishments as frequently as they are admonished for their failures.

When you establish clearly specified objectives and rewards for each of your team members you create an environment for achievement.

People like recognition.

Sandy was recently hired to manage a retail operation in a resort town in Southern California. One day during a discussion with a sales clerk she made an off-handed comment, "...and I'll give you a gold star if you can sell these slowly moving T-shirts."

During the following week the sales clerk sold every T-shirt. He met with Sandy and asked for his gold star. She went to a nearby drug store, bought a package of gold star stickers and placed one next to the sales clerk's name on the time card rack.

Much to her surprise, Sandy was approached by other people on her sales staff who asked how they could earn gold stars. Pretty soon the gold stars became part of a tangible recognition system and the overall performance of the store increased dramatically.

When Sandy told me this story she said, "I never imagined that a fifty cent package of gold stars would have this kind of impact on my employees."

Good things happen from good reinforcement.

The form of recognition for improved performance is far less important than the significance it is given by your team members.

Cash awards are nice and certainly have their place in rewarding accomplishment. You will find, however, that public acknowledgement of achievement is the key element in inspiring your team members to grow and strive for greater performance.

TRUTH OR CONSEQUENCES?

Every company has pieces that 'don't work' from time to time. You need to utilize the functions that do work and apply them to critical operations while you are fixing the pieces that don't work.

Use the Texas Four Step to attack the areas that aren't performing up to your expectations.

1. **Establish the benchmark.**

   Evaluate what you are doing.

   Is it worth doing at all?

   Do you and your team need to change your skills, your attitudes or your behavior?

2. **Set goals.**

   Shoot for something new and exciting.

   Establish short term goals your team can hit.

3. **Create strategies.**

   Search for new ideas that may run counter to your experiences.

   Demolish old ideas and rules which aren't working.

   Look for new ways to do the job - apply simple ideas on a consistent basis.

   Start again.

4. **Monitor results.**

   Give ongoing visibility to your progress.

   Promote success.

Achieve the impossible.

About the Author

Mark Kelly is the founder of TASC management consultants, a consulting resource for a wide spectrum of private and public corporations and small businesses throughout the United States.

His firm teaches professional managers and business owners how to maximize the results of their efforts through tools designed to enhance their planning, goal setting, accountability, empowerment, and communication skills.

He has an MBA from George Washington University and undergraduate degrees in English Literature (Clemson University) and Business Administration (University of South Carolina).

Prior to entering the management consulting profession he was the president of public companies in both the electronics and government services fields. He has extensive experience in domestic and international management issues.

He is the creator and presenter of numerous management and sales development workshops and seminars. He is sought after throughout the country as a public speaker on team building, leadership, communication and employee development.

His management consulting practice is located in Southern California. For more information on the tools presented in this book, please contact:

TASC management consultants
26542 Mimosa Lane
Mission Viejo, Ca 92691
(714) 830-8821

ORDER FORM

Fax Orders:	(714) 830-8436
Mail Orders:	*Thresher Press*
	22365 El Toro Road, #344
	Lake Forest, CA 92630
Phone Orders:	1-800-365-8841

Please send The Manager's Toolbox to:

• **Name:** _____

• **Company Name:** _____

• **Address:** _____

• **City:** _____

• **State:** _____ ZIP Code: _____

• **Telephone:** ( ) _____

Order quantity:	_____
Price per copy:	$ 11.95
Extended price:	$_____
Sales tax *:	$_____
Subtotal:	$_____
Shipping **:	$_____
Order Total:	$_____

*   For shipments to California, please add 7.75% sales tax.

** Please add $2.00 for the first book; $.50 for each
     additional book

Payment:

☐ **Check**

☐ **Credit Card**

    Card number: _____

    Name on card: _____

    Expiration date: _____

☐ **Please send my complimentary copy of
    Mark Kelly's quarterly TASC NOTES.**